LEGACY

LEGACY PATRONS

Eleanor "Snooky" and M. H. "Blake" Blakemore,
  Co-chairs, LEGACY Campaign

Atkinson and Company, Albuquerque

BF Foundation, Santa Fe

Marjorie and Robert Beck

Berry and Dianne Cash

Sarah and Ben Crane

Charles and Valerie Diker

Barbara and Bud Hoover

Rollin and Mary Ella King

Mr. and Mrs. Dennis Lyon

Ted and Betsy Rogers

Drs. Mark and Kathleen Sublette

Eugene V. & Clare E. Thaw Charitable Trust, Santa Fe

Lore Thorpe

John and Samantha Williams

LEGACY

SOUTHWEST INDIAN ART AT THE SCHOOL OF AMERICAN RESEARCH

DUANE ANDERSON, EDITOR

SCHOOL OF AMERICAN RESEARCH PRESS ❖ SANTA FE ❖ NEW MEXICO

School of American Research Press
Post Office Box 2188
Santa Fe, New Mexico 87504-2188

Director of Publications: Joan K. O'Donnell
Editor: Jo Ann Baldinger
Art Director: Deborah Flynn Post
Major Photography: Addison Doty
Printer: CS Graphics, Singapore

Library of Congress Cataloging-in-Publication Data:
Legacy : Southwest Indian art at the School of American
        Research / Duane Anderson, editor.
          p.   cm.
        Includes bibliographical references.
        ISBN 0-933452-54-3 (cloth). --   ISBN 0-933452-
        57-8 (pbk.)
        1. School of American Research (Santa Fe, N.M.).
        Indian Arts Research Center--Art collections--
        Catalogs. 2. School of American Research (Santa Fe,
        N.M.) Indian Arts Research Center--Ethnological
        collections--Catalogs. 3. Indian pottery--Southwest,
        New--Catalogs. 4. Indian textile fabrics--Southwest,
        New--Catalogs. 5. Indians of North America--
        Southwest, New--Antiquities--Catalogs.
        6. Southwest, New--Antiquities--Catalogs.
        I. Anderson, Duane, 1943-
        E78.S7L44 1999
        704.03'97'007478956--dc21   98-36554
                                                  CIP

Copyright ©1999 by the School of American Research.
        All rights reserved. Library of Congress Catalog Card
        Number 98-36554. International Standard Book
        Numbers 0-933452-54-3 (cloth); 0-933452-56-X
        (limited edition); 0-933452-57-8 (paper). First edition.

Front and back covers: San Ildefonso Polychrome jar by
        Maria Martinez and Julian Martinez, 1926. IAF.1166.
        Photographs by Addison Doty.

Printed and bound in Singapore.

To all those who created
the Indian art legacy
at the School of American Research.

CONTENTS

FOREWORD

The celebration of legacy is appropriate, and the celebration is necessarily spiritual. The greatest gifts are those that come down from our ancestors, for they bind us to our origins. We are original, aboriginal beings; the air we breathe was breathed by our grandmothers and grandfathers.

> And, furthermore, yonder in the west
> You who are my father, bear,
> You who are life-giving society chief;
> Bringing your medicine,
> You will make your road come hither,
> Where lies my white shell bowl,
> Four times making your road come in,
> Watch over my spring.
> When you sit down quietly
> We shall be one person.
> —Zuni

In this prayer the speaker invokes the ancestral bear in order to appropriate the bear's curing powers. In the last line is accomplished the ultimate communion between ancestor and descendant: they become one. The invocation is ancient, and the communion is sacred and profound, a bonding intrinsic and indispensable in the expression of the Native spirit. It is pervasive in Southwest Indian art. In Pueblo tradition the breath is given out, then it is retrieved in the bowl of the hands and returned to the mouth. Food is not taken but that a small portion is first set apart for the ancestral spirits.

The legacy celebrated here is valuable beyond telling. Indeed, the notion of value—measured worth in our customary way of thinking—is nearly irrelevant in the presence of these things. They are informed with sacred aspect, and they exist in a dimension in which other things do not exist. We can only be grateful for them; we can only know them for their own sake. We extend to them honor, belief, wonder, and delight, for that offering is appropriate. And first and last, we must approach them—appropriate them to our experience—in the appropriate way.

What informs this bowl, this basket, this weaving, this painting? It is always, I believe, a totality greater than the sum of its parts. There is a fourth dimension of eternity, an essence of earth and sky, a rhythm of ancient breathing. I have a silver and turquoise ring, given to me by my father. He had worn it for years. When he gave it to me he said, "The man who made this ring believed that, by looking at this stone, his eyesight grew stronger." My father believed that his sight was improved in the same way. I believe that mine is. This is not to say that belief in itself raises art to a sacred level. It is to say that in many of the greatest works of art there is an essential element of cultural tenure, a tradition evolved over untold generations. The man who made my ring had an investment of perhaps thirty thousand years in the landscape of this continent. That is worth something. That worth is reflected in the ring. It *is* the ring, and it is the bowl, the basket, the weaving, the painting.

Those who behold this legacy will regard it variously. And each beholder will regard it rightly. It is homage to ancestors. It is heritage. It is a tribute to human creativity. It is inspiration, fulfillment, and promise. It is the reliquary of a primordial cathedral, it is that which engenders inspiration, contemplation, and, yes, love—the love of beauty and of the continuum of human being. When we breathe in the presence of these things, let us give thanks, and in our hands return our breath to ourselves, that we may enter into communion with space and time and eternity.

N. Scott Momaday (Kiowa)

PREFACE

For many years the School of American Research (SAR) has considered producing a special book that would highlight some of the beautiful and intriguing objects from the collection of our Indian Arts Research Center (IARC). The celebration of SAR's ninetieth anniversary (1997–98) seemed a fitting occasion for such a volume, especially since 1998 also marks the twentieth year of the IARC. *Legacy* thus commemorates a double anniversary.

The IARC's collection of Indian art of the American Southwest is one of the most spectacular in the world. It comprises more than eleven thousand objects, including pottery, baskets, paintings, textiles, jewelry, katsinas, and clothing, and represents most of the Southwest's Native American tribes. Housed in a secure, climate-controlled environment, with fully automated imaging and data management systems, the collection is a superb resource for Native American artists, for scholars, and for the many members of the public who visit the beautiful Pueblo-style building for docent-guided tours. Today, the IARC maintains a leadership position in the Indian arts field through its innovative programs for visiting Native American artists, the Harvey W. Branigar, Jr., Native American Fellowship, the Ron and Susan Dubin Native American Artist Fellowship, annual artist convocations, and Indian art publications.

Early in the planning of this book, we decided to emphasize the historical and aesthetic legacy of the collection. This led us to explore the web of relationships that has developed over time among Native American artists, patrons, benefactors, scholars, SAR staff members, and others whose interaction with the collection has continued to enrich and enhance its significance.

During the past century, many Native American crafts have been transformed into "art" in the Western sense. At the same time, Indian artists have struggled to maintain their unique cultural traditions. This context provides a fertile field for studying the processes of creativity and change as well as the results of these processes. The ninety objects featured in this volume have been selected not only to provide a feast for the eye but also to stimulate consideration of how they were created and why they were collected, and to suggest some interesting contrasts with today's approaches to Indian art and new artistic initiatives.

This book represents but one contribution to the protean legacy that began in Santa Fe in the 1920s, when a small group of visionaries founded the Indian Arts Fund for the purpose of preserving important objects of Native American art. As SAR moves into its tenth decade, we hope this *Legacy* volume will also serve as a reaffirmation of that vision and a tribute to Indian artists, past and present, and to those benefactors who helped to preserve the aesthetic heritage of the Native American Southwest.

Douglas W. Schwartz
President and Chief Executive Officer
School of American Research

Douglas W. Schwartz in the IARC's main vault.

LEGACY

A LIVING LEGACY

Duane Anderson and Michael J. Hering

A legacy is a gift from an ancestor, something handed down across time and space, and through the generations. It draws its significance from how and by whom it was created and acquired, and why it was preserved and passed on. Any legacy changes over time, taking on new meanings with each new context and each succeeding generation.

The pieces featured in this book are held in the collections of the Indian Arts Research Center at the School of American Research in Santa Fe, New Mexico. They represent the work of Native American artisans who for centuries have fashioned objects that were both utilitarian and beautiful. They also represent a legacy that reflects the skills, traditions, and enthusiasms of the items' makers, their descendants, their users, their collectors, and their admirers.

The legacy story of the School of American Research collections began in 1922, when a small group of Santa Fe art patrons, wishing to ensure the preservation of the traditional arts of the Pueblo villages of New Mexico, began to acquire examples of fine old Indian pottery. Incorporating in 1924 as the Indian Arts Fund, the group soon expanded the scope of its collections to include baskets, textiles, paintings, and other art categories from all the Native peoples of the Southwest, as well as selected items from other western Indian groups. These objects form the core of what is today one of world's premier collections of Southwest Indian art.

Founded in 1907 by Edgar Lee Hewett, the School of American Research (SAR) is a nonprofit center for advanced study in anthropology and American Indian arts. The preparation of this book is part of a larger project intended to commemorate SAR's ninetieth birthday year. The volume focuses on ninety items from our collection, each of which provides some insight into the relationships that developed over the last ninety years among Native American artists, collectors, patrons, and researchers. It stands as an offering from SAR to the makers who created this legacy and the admirers of Indian art who preserved it.

The legacy story told here unfolds gradually, as individual examples from the collection are discussed. We asked fourteen renowned scholars to contribute their expertise to the writing of this book; they also participated in the selection process. Each object has its own story to tell, a narrative based on our understanding of how, when, and, in some cases, by whom it was made, and for what purpose. Scholarly research on the collection and its active use by Native Americans today continue to add meaning and historic value to the objects and provide an ever-expanding source of inspiration and knowledge. We often know something about the individuals who collected these objects as well, and this information can further enrich our understanding and appreciation.

The main administration building of the School of American Research, built in 1926–27 as the home of Elizabeth and Martha White.

The History of the Indian Arts Fund

IAF pots were stored in the basement of the Museum of Fine Arts in the 1920s.

Anyone who has visited the vaults at the Indian Arts Research Center will appreciate the challenge we faced in selecting ninety "representative" items to be featured in this book. There are so many worthy candidates, and so many ways an object can be a bearer of a legacy.

One characteristic shared by many of the pieces is that they were collected by the loving hands of members of the Indian Arts Fund (IAF). According to its own origin story, the IAF came into being in 1922 after an old Zuni Ashiwi Polychrome pot was accidentally broken at a dinner party at the home of Elizabeth Shepley Sergeant in the village of Tesuque, just north of Santa Fe. Concerned that fine examples of traditional Pueblo arts were disappearing, Sergeant and her guests that evening were inspired to form what they called the Pueblo Pottery Fund, a group that dedicated itself to acquiring the finest pieces of traditional pottery and using them to encourage contemporary Indian artists.

Two years later the group expanded the scope of its collecting and incorporated as the Indian Arts Fund, whose stated purpose was "to revive the Arts and Crafts of the Indians by giving them free access to the choicest specimens of their tribal art." IAF members were among the most knowledgeable and active collectors of their time in the Southwest. In addition to Elizabeth Sergeant, a writer, Indian rights activist, and member of the New Mexico Association on Indian Affairs, they included Elizabeth White, patron of Indian arts, Indian rights activist, and popular hostess to Santa Fe's lively community of artists, writers, and intellectuals; Kenneth M. Chapman, curator, artist, and a leading authority on Pueblo ceramics; Andrew Dasburg, modernist painter and member of the Taos Society of Artists, known as the "father of American cubism"; pioneer Southwestern archaeologist Jesse L. Nusbaum; novelist and arts patron Mary Austin; poet Alice Corbin Henderson, a founder and editor of the avant-garde magazine *Poetry*; Mabel Dodge Luhan, the writer and Taos hostess perhaps best known for bringing Georgia O'Keeffe and D. H. Lawrence, among others, to New Mexico; Alfred Vincent Kidder, whose excavations at Pecos Pueblo earned him the title of "dean of Southwestern archaeologists"; Sylvanus G. Morley, eminent Maya scholar and later director of the School of American Research; and Harry P. Mera, physician and author of dozens of important studies on Southwestern Indian arts.

In the early years the collection was kept in IAF members' homes. By 1925, Edgar Lee Hewett, founder and director of the School of American Research and of New Mexico's state museum system, was providing space for the collection in the basement of the Museum of Fine Arts on the Santa Fe plaza. In 1931 the Indian Arts Fund collection was moved to the basement of the newly constructed and independently financed Laboratory of Anthropology, where it remained for many years.

In the 1920s and 1930s, Hewett was actively pursuing his own agenda of support for Native American arts by working to improve traditional arts and crafts at the pueblos and to develop markets for them. IAF members shared Hewett's goal: in 1922 they were instrumental in establishing the first Southwest Indian Fair, forerunner of today's Santa Fe Indian Market. As the IAF

Artist and scholar Kenneth M. Chapman completed some of the earliest and most comprehensive studies of Pueblo pottery design while he was a curator of the IAF collection.

collection grew, scholars like Harry Mera and Kenneth Chapman began to make their mark. In the 1930s they published pioneering studies of the collection that are now recognized as classics in the field of Native American art.

In 1972 members of the Indian Arts Fund board, chaired by Alton R. Packard, approached SAR president Douglas W. Schwartz and offered to donate the entire IAF collection of 4,280 items to the School. Dr. Schwartz accepted the challenge and took steps to endow a new Indian Arts Research Center (IARC), construct a suitable building on the SAR campus, and develop an active program to ensure that the collection would be used by Native American artists and interested scholars and would be accessible to the public. The original IARC building, encompassing Vault One, was completed in 1978 with a grant from Perrine Dixon McCune in honor of her late husband, Marshall L. McCune. Vault Two and the adjoining offices were added in 1986.

Since the IARC opened in 1978, the focus of the collection has narrowed to the greater Southwest in the historic and contemporary periods (1540 to the present). But the collection also contains several outstanding examples of works from Native American groups who are historic neighbors and trading partners of the peoples of the Southwest. Some of these are included in this volume (see pages 93, 201, 202, 208, and 210). Under SAR's stewardship the collection has grown to eleven thousand objects representing forty-eight tribes, thirty-eight of which live in the Southwest. During the past two decades generous artists, patrons, and benefactors have contributed art objects and the financial resources needed to expand the collection and achieve a balance within different artistic categories.

Legacy Stories

San Ildefonso potter Maria Martinez, 1946.

Many objects from the original Indian Arts Fund collection carry stories that define and underline the legacy theme of this book. One of these items, known as IAF Number 1, is the restored pottery vessel that was broken at Elizabeth Sergeant's dinner party in 1922. This rare pot (see page 21) not only inspired the formation of the Indian Arts Fund collection but has also become the "type specimen" of Ashiwi Poly-chrome, a regional Zuni style of the early 1700s. Another remarkable piece is the Chief White Antelope blanket (page 99), a beautifully woven Navajo wearing blanket recovered from the mas-sacre field at Sand Creek, Colorado, in 1864. This unique and well-preserved textile richly illustrates how an object can bear multiple meanings, hold-ing significance in different ways for differ-ent groups of people. To members of the Southern Cheyenne community, it is a potent piece of history, a tangible reminder of their great chief White Antelope and of the tragedy of the Sand Creek massacre. To textile scientists and art historians, it is a repository of technical and methodological infor-mation, with much to tell about Navajo design styles, dyes, materials, weaving techniques, and inter-tribal commerce during New Mexico's Territorial days. To Navajo weavers, its unparalleled work-manship is both an inspiration and a challenge.

Several of the pottery vessels chosen for this volume represent a different sort of legacy, self-conscious revivals of design styles in use before European contact. The triangular, black-tipped feather motifs on the Zia storage jar pictured on page 47, for instance, can be traced back to Puname Polychrome pottery produced two hundred years earlier (see page 51). Precontact fine-line designs reappear in the pottery of Lucy Lewis of Acoma Pueblo (page 32). Other pottery design motifs were inspired by rock art. For example, Julian Martinez, husband of San Ildefonso potter Maria Martinez, is believed to have adapted the *awanyu* or "water serpent" motif shown on page 7 from a petroglyph at Tsirege, a Pueblo IV site located in the mountains just west of San Ildefonso Pueblo near the modern city of Los Alamos.

The effects of contact between different cultures are reflected in such diverse items as the Cochiti figurines that poke fun at outsiders (see page 53) and the textile work of Navajo medicine man Hosteen Klah (page 107), whose rugs depicting ceremonial drypaintings were designed to record these ephemeral creations in a more permanent form. Many of the IARC's paintings on paper (pages 70–93) depict cultural contact between Native artists and Euro-American patrons or buyers, as do the Mojave figurines from the Lower Colorado River (page 63). The latter, made exclusively for tourists, provide a unique record of the early-twentieth-century dress and symbolism of this culturally rich but artistically underappreciated group from southwestern Arizona.

Many of the *Legacy* objects are tied to the activities of prominent individuals in the region— Indians as well as their Anglo patrons. Crescencio Martinez from San Ildefonso Pueblo (see page 72) influenced a whole generation of painters from several pueblos whose works are well represented in the SAR collection. Patrons from Santa Fe and Taos, including Kenneth Chapman, Andrew Dasburg, Dorothy Dunn, Edgar Lee Hewett, and

Southwestern archaeologist Marjorie Lambert, ca. 1935.

Mabel Dodge Luhan, among others, encouraged, supported, and influenced Indian painters such as Martinez, Velino Shije Herrera, Fred Kabotie, and Awa Tsireh. Anglo patrons purchased art, provided studio space, and publicized Native American arts nationally and internationally through exhibits, books, and magazine articles.

Over the years the SAR collection has been greatly enriched through gifts and bequests from such individuals as Elizabeth White, Sallie Wagner, Marjorie Lambert, Rick Dillingham, Henry Galbraith, Leonora Paloheimo, Margaret Moses, the Honorable and Mrs. Oliver Seth, and Ruth Holmwood. The most significant "life series" of Native American artworks was assembled over a period of years by Sallie Wagner. An Honorary Life Member of SAR's Board of Managers, Wagner donated her collection of 270 works by the Navajo painter Beatien Yazz, spanning almost sixty years, to the IARC in 1983. Her gift illustrates dramatically the great significance of the contribution of one individual to the legacy preserved and curated by SAR.

Sallie Wagner and customers at Wide Ruins Trading Post, ca. 1945. Wagner ran the Arizona post from 1938 to 1948.

A Legacy for the Future

In the early decades of the twentieth century, the Indian Arts Fund and Edgar Lee Hewett and his associates directed their efforts toward preserving and reviving Native American arts. They did so by collecting fine work from the past and encouraging artistic production in the present through commissions, a willingness to pay higher prices for objects, and the development of outlets such as the Santa Fe Indian Fair and its successor, the Santa Fe Indian Market. Since its establishment twenty years ago, the Indian Arts Research Center has expanded its focus from collecting and curating to include a number of programs intended to foster collaboration and cooperation with Southwestern Indian artists. At the same

Participants in the Micaceous Pottery Artists Convocation, 1994. From left: Lydia Pesata (Jicarilla Apache), Dawn Antelope (Taos Pueblo), Christine McHorse (Navajo), Edna Romero (Taos), Lonnie Vigil (Nambe), Felipe Ortega (Jicarilla Apache), Sharon Dryflower Reyna (Taos), Angie Yazzie (Taos), Anthony Durand (Picuris), Juanita DuBray (Taos).

time, it is investing greater effort in studying and documenting the creative process. There has been a shift of emphasis from "arts" to "artists" in our contemporary work.

The Artists Convocation program at SAR was designed with these goals in mind. Once a year, ten accomplished artists working in a particular medium are invited to gather at the Santa Fe campus for three days of discussions aimed at assessing the current status and future directions of their art. Each participant brings a work created especially for the convocation, and these pieces are purchased and added to the Indian Arts Research Center collection. Shawn Tafoya's Pueblo embroidered breechcloth (see page 123) and Mary Holiday Black's Navajo basket (page 149) are but two examples of the work produced for these special gatherings. Convocation themes change each year, ensuring that all categories of the collection receive the attention they deserve.

Native American artists and students study the IARC collections. Clockwise from top: potters from Santa Ana Pueblo, 1990; Navajo weavers from Ramah, 1988; Mescalero Apache basketmaking students, 1988.

Corresponding research and conservation themes serve as focal points for many of the IARC's other activities during the year. The Ron and Susan Dubin Native American Artist Fellowship provides Indian artists time to study the collection while creating their own work in the multipurpose Dubin Artist Studio adjoining the IARC. During their tenure, Dubin fellows work with IARC staff to plan future convocations that relate to their own areas of expertise.

Another fellowship opportunity is provided by the BF Foundation in honor of the late Harvey W. Branigar, Jr. Each year one Harvey W. Branigar, Jr., Native American Fellow spends nine months at the IARC working with collections management, conservation, and public access projects in preparation for a career in museums and cultural centers.

The Native American Arts Education program brings more than 250 Indian artists, elders, students, and children annually to the SAR campus to tour and study the collections. Program participants gain both a better appreciation for the artistic work of the past and the inspiration needed to stimulate their imaginations and explore new frontiers in their own creative work. At the same time, these visitors add significantly to our understanding of particular objects in the

Ron Martinez Looking Elk (Isleta and Taos Pueblos), the 1997–98 Branigar Fellow.

Kevin Navasie (Hopi), the 1997 Dubin Artist Fellow.

collections through their comments, observations, recollections, and personal experiences as makers and mentors.

The collections are also shared with a wider public through the publication of Indian arts books. Scholarly and popular works about the IARC collections include books by Duane Anderson, Jonathan Batkin, J. J. Brody, Kenneth Chapman, Rick Dillingham, Jill McKeever Furst, Francis H. Harlow, Kate Peck Kent, Harry P. Mera, Sallie Wagner, and Andrew H. Whiteford (see Selected Bibliography). These scholars have added greatly to our understanding of broad anthropological and art historical topics and have given us insight into how particular traditions are perpetuated. In *Acoma & Laguna Pottery*, for example, Rick Dillingham includes contemporary works by Wanda Aragon and Rosemary Chino Garcia, whose creations are inspired by earlier generations of potters. Other books are in preparation covering aspects of the pottery, jewelry, textile, and basketry collections. The collections are also made available on loan to museums around the world for use in exhibitions and interpretive programs. And here in Santa Fe, thousands of people have visited the collections on docent-guided tours since the Indian Arts Research Center opened its doors in 1978.

From left, Jonathan Batkin, Charlie Perkins, Margaret Perkins, Duane Anderson, Peter Babcock.

A Tour of the Indian Arts Research Center

The Indian Arts Research Center's main vault.

Visitors walking through the heavy doors of the Indian Arts Research Center's main vault are immediately confronted with an unforgettable image: four thousand of the finest historic-period pottery vessels from throughout the American Southwest, displayed in tier upon tier of open shelving in a two-story, five-thousand-square-foot space. The shelves directly in front of the entrance are densely packed with pottery from Acoma Pueblo, including large eighteenth- and nineteenth-century dough bowls and storage jars along with pieces by more contemporary potters such as the late Lucy Lewis and her daughters.

The shelves to the right contain a large assemblage of pottery by the internationally known San Ildefonso potters Maria and Julian Martinez, as well as selected works by other members of their family, including their son, PoPovi Da, and granddaughter, Barbara Gonzales. Across the parquet floor, more thick wooden shelves support masterpieces from the pueblos of Laguna, Santa Ana, Zia, and Santo Domingo. Nearby are huge polychrome storage jars from San Ildefonso, enormous red-on-tan bowls from San Juan, and polished black wares from Santa Clara. There are also vessels from Tesuque Pueblo, old cooking and storage jars from Taos and Picuris, and glittering examples of the micaceous art pottery that has recently emerged in the northern Rio Grande Pueblo villages.

At the far end of the vault, large figurines from Cochiti Pueblo peer out from the layered shelves. Some depict Italian opera singers, made in the late nineteenth century after a delegation of Cochiti men traveled by rail to New York City, where completely new forms of arts and entertainment clearly made a lasting impression. Other Cochiti figurines from around 1900 feature tongue-in-cheek interpretations of Catholic priests, cowboys, and Anglo tourists. On a higher shelf are early examples of Helen Cordero's celebrated "storyteller" figurines dating to 1964, when she started a new tradition at the suggestion of folk art collector Alexander Girard.

Off to the left of the Cochiti materials are hundreds of fine pottery vessels from Santo Domingo Pueblo, including works by contemporary potters Robert Tenorio and Andrew Pacheco. To the right, a small vault contains an outstanding collection of Navajo and Pueblo jewelry. "Old pawn" and silverwork pieces from Route 66 days twinkle on the shelves alongside contemporary Santo Domingo and Zuni works created by participants in SAR's recent Mosaic Jewelry Artists Convocation.

A new adventure awaits visitors on the vault's second floor, where the collection of rare Navajo and Pueblo textiles is housed. With nearly a thousand pieces representing a time span of three hundred years, this one of the largest and most significant collections of its kind. A few steps away, large drawers contain Pueblo weavings and embroideries, and row upon row of belts, sashes, moccasins, and other articles of clothing. Displayed on the opposite side of the vault are a number of items from the collection of over thirteen hundred paintings on paper produced by early-twentieth-century artists from various Southwestern tribes.

Other cabinets on the second floor house an extensive collection of drums, rattles, rasps, and other musical instruments from many Indian communities. Large drawers hold elegant deerskin dresses made by the Arapahos of the southern Great Plains, as well as garments of the Jicarilla and Mescalero Apaches. Beautifully decorated Western Apache saddlebags, used to carry food and supplies, remind us of the utilitarian nature of so many of these magnificent objects. An elaborate Cheyenne war shield and a pair of cradleboards of the Kiowa and Ute tribes adorn the nearby walls.

Moving to the head of the stairs, visitors encounter the outstanding collection of katsina dolls, including 240 items recently acquired through a bequest of the late Ruth Holmwood, former owner of the Kachina House Gallery in Santa Fe. (Katsina, the spelling used in this volume, reflects the Hopi pronunciation, cot-SEE-nah.) Most of the katsina doll carvings are from

the pueblos of Hopi and Zuni, and many are rare pieces from early in the twentieth century. Among the hundreds of spirits represented are Shalakos (Chief katsinas), Salimopias (Warriors), Hututu (Rain Priests of the North), and a variety of fearsome-looking Ogres. The dolls are important in Pueblo religion and are used to instruct children in the culture of the tribe, but they are generally not regarded as sacred objects. Nevertheless, the katsina shelves are covered up on days when uninitiated young tribal members visit the vault.

Just when visitors are showing signs of sensory overload, the tour guide announces that it is now time to go and explore "the other vault." Almost in unison, everyone gasps, "There's more?"

Vault Two is somewhat smaller—only three thousand square feet—and is laid out like the nave of a small church, with chapels on both sides. Baskets are on the left, pottery from Zuni and Hopi villages is on the right, and a large assemblage of Mojave figurines and effigy vessels is tucked away behind the shelf containing the old Zuni pottery. The walls of the dome-shaped apse at the far end of the room are hung with examples of the tabletas Pueblo women wear on their heads during certain dances. In the center of the apse, a huge sparkling black pot made by Nambé potter Lonnie Vigil occupies a place of honor on an oaken pedestal (see page 69). A gift from Indian Arts Fund patrons in 1995, it represents one of the finest examples of the new micaceous art pottery tradition ever produced.

Vault Two.

The Legacy Lives On

This book is a tribute to Native American arts and artists and to the many individuals who have been instrumental in the acquisition, care, and use of the collections over the last seventy-five years. Talented artists, knowledgeable scholars, discerning collectors, capable board members, and dedicated staff members have pooled their energies to create something very special at the School of American Research. Today the Indian Arts Research Center is a meeting ground for Native American artists and for scholars from around the world, a safe haven for thousands of priceless objects, and an unparalleled place of inspiration and contemplation for members of the public. It is a place where legacy not only lives, but is reborn and reconfigured with the passing of each new day.

Textile scholar Kate Peck Kent (right) with Barbara Stanislavsky, 1981.

POTTERY

Ashiwi Polychrome Jar

Zuni Pueblo, ca. 1680
IAF.1
Height: 22.9cm Diameter: 33cm
Acquired in 1922

This three-hundred-year-old Zuni water jar was the inspiration for the formation of the Indian Arts Fund (IAF) collection. In 1922 it was dropped and broken at the Tesuque home of Elizabeth Shepley Sergeant shortly before the arrival of her dinner guests, Harry P. Mera, Wesley Bradfield, and Kenneth Chapman—all, like their hostess, admirers and collectors of traditional Pueblo pottery. The incident provoked a discussion of the fact that the large, functional styles of pottery were being replaced by utilitarian containers made of other materials and by smaller pots produced especially for the tourist market. That evening the group decided to form the Pueblo Pottery Fund, precursor of the IAF. Its mission was to collect and preserve the finest examples of Indian art and to use the collections to encourage Native peoples of the Southwest to continue working with traditional styles and techniques.

This pot is the type specimen (that is, the standard to which all others are compared) of the early historic period of Zuni Pueblo pottery known as Ashiwi Polychrome (ca. 1680–1750) and is one of only about fifteen such complete vessels in existence. The base is concave, to facilitate being carried on the head. The underbody walls flare outward in a graceful midbody bulge, creating a low center of gravity that tapers inward to form the shoulder. There is no neck on the vessel; the shoulder continues to the rim.

Similar in shape to Puname Polychrome from Zia, Ako Polychrome from Acoma, and Payupki Polychrome made at the Hopi villages, Ashiwi Polychrome was probably influenced by pottery from the Keres-speaking pueblos of the Rio Grande, particularly Zia. This influence spread westward before and after the Pueblo Revolt of 1680. Ashiwi Polychrome is known for its white kaolinite background slip, with the overall design of the pot outlined in black and motifs painted in deep red and black. The base, rim, and interior rim are red. Dominant motifs include abstract feathers and birds, geometric elements such as stepped sections and triangles, and open "eyes." According to Zuni potter Milford Nahohai, "It is fitting for a water jar of this period to be painted with feather and bird images, because birds are the messengers to the gods to carry our prayers for rain." *Michael J. Hering*

Founding members of the Indian Arts Fund, ca. 1964.
From left: Andrew Dasburg, Amelia Elizabeth White,
Kenneth Chapman, Jesse Nusbaum.

San Ildefonso Polychrome Water Jar

Toñita Peña
San Ildefonso Pueblo, 1880
IAF.23
Height: 27.9cm   Diameter: 33cm
Acquired in 1923

San Ildefonso was a small community of thirty-seven households in 1880, and the demand for serviceable pottery was met by a handful of skilled potters. Among them was a woman whose baptismal name was Maria Antonia Peña, and whose Tewa name meant Yellow Deer. (She should not be confused with the famous painter Tonita Peña, two generations her junior.)

This rare example of Peña's work, one of the finest traditional San Ildefonso water jars in the Indian Arts Fund collection, was acquired from a Santa Fe curio dealer in 1923. Kenneth Chapman illustrated isolated elements of its design in his landmark book, *The Pottery of San Ildefonso Pueblo*, but he never attributed it to Peña. This is surprising, because the maker's identity became known to him in 1920 when he acquired a fragmentary storage jar that was clearly made by the same individual.

Here Peña painted marvelous birds with fantails, walking in procession around the circumference of the pot. This style of decoration was utterly revolutionary, not only at San Ildefonso, but at any of the pueblos. At San Ildefonso, these renderings of birds may have been among the first. At other pueblos, birds were depicted as static, either enclosed within geometric elements or perched in foliage.

Peña's pots were painted not only by her but also by her daughter Anastacia, her grand-nephew Alfredo Montoya (one of San Ildefonso's pioneer watercolor painters), and possibly others. Regardless of the painter, many of her pots are decorated with walking birds, and several have depictions of hummingbirds feeding on nectar. Stepped elements, which represent clouds, are another common motif.

One of the most unusual technical details of this pot is the use of two different red paints: one decidedly orange, the other closer to true red. This is an extremely rare treatment on San Ildefonso Polychrome pottery today, and it may be peculiar to this potter's work. On the other hand, it may have been a common practice at the time the pot was made. Despite its relatively late date of manufacture, there are very few examples with which it can be compared. *Jonathan Batkin*

Kiua Polychrome Jar

Santo Domingo Pueblo, ca. 1860–70
IAF.340
Height: 40.6cm   Diameter: 48.2cm
Acquired in 1925

The eighteenth century was a time of great change for the pottery of the eastern Keres-speaking pueblos of Cochiti, Santo Domingo, and San Felipe. Until 1700, all three had produced pots decorated with a pigment containing a lead-oxide base, which melted during the firing and resolidified to a glassy, true-glaze finish. By 1700, however, after the turmoil of the Pueblo Revolt and the Spanish reconquest, the glaze-paint technique was lost, and the three villages had to find a new way to decorate their pottery. San Felipe simply stopped decorating pottery altogether, producing a succession of dark gray or polished red styles. Santo Domingo and Cochiti switched to an entirely different pigment for the black lines. Their teachers were the Tewa Indians with whom they had lived as refugees during the most troublesome years, and the pigment they learned to use is guaco, a vegetal paint.

The potters also adopted a variety of Tewa design ideas, so that some Keres vessels from the late eighteenth century look as though they could have come from the Tewa pueblos. The distinction is easily made, however, on the basis of differences in tempering material in the clay, the use of different slip materials, and, after around 1800, the black Keres and red Tewa rim tops. In what

can be termed a ceramics renaissance at both Cochiti and Santo Domingo, the potters became thorough masters of their new technique for painted designs. Perhaps their most striking accomplishments are the large storage jars constructed at both villages.

This jar, from just after the mid-nineteenth century, is a superb example of the pottery type that bears the Indian name for Santa Domingo: Kiua Polychrome. The designs seen here all have traditional roots. The geometric pattern on the neck occurs on numerous bowls and jars made at both villages since the middle of the eighteenth century. Lines of diamonds in vertical bands on the midbody hark back to precontact times in many parts of the Pueblo world. The spirals with triangular embellishments likewise have prehistoric roots and occur in numerous variations, especially during the period 1750 to 1850. More subtle features include the bottom-to-top pattern cleavage at one place around the circumference, an extreme manifestation of the often-employed "'ceremonial break'" in encircling framing lines and path lines. The orange-red band below the design area is wider than the blood-red bands found at that same location on Tewa pots. *Francis H. Harlow*

Woman at Santo Domingo Pueblo, ca. 1915.

Cochiti Polychrome Bowl

Cochiti Pueblo, ca. 1890–1910
IAF.380
Height: 45.7cm   Diameter: 55.9cm
Acquired in 1925

By 1880 most of the pottery being made at Cochiti Pueblo consisted of figurines and effigy vessels. Bowls and jars were rare, and given the wear and tear that accompanied everyday use, few pieces of this size and quality found their way into museum collections. This particularly large Cochiti Polychrome bowl, with its red underbody, light slip, and fine-line decoration, has been described by scholar Frank Harlow as delicate, complex, and busy.

   The use of sacred figurative motifs on utilitarian pottery or on pieces made for sale or trade was rare among other Rio Grande pueblos but quite common at Cochiti. Bowls, jars, and figurative forms alike were covered with delicate and intricate designs, many of which were naturalistic and unmistakably ceremonial. The flaring rim and framing lines with pendant designs were also distinct features of Cochiti ceramics. The pendant design with rain cloud motifs seen here on the inside rim was not, however, a common feature. A ceremonial line break was characteristically made in Cochiti banding lines, but such breaks on the interior of the rim were atypical. The elaborate, symmetrical, four-part design centered in the interior is unusual in pottery made for everyday use. On the other hand, the interiors of ceremonial bowls were usually decorated with both geometric and figurative designs associated with rain and fertility. *Barbara A. Babcock*

Santa Ana Polychrome Dough Bowl

Santa Ana Pueblo, ca. 1860
IAF.522
Height: 24cm   Diameter: 44.5cm
Acquired in 1926

The bold red designs outlined in black on this large bowl instantly identify it as a product of Santa Ana Pueblo. The distinctive Santa Ana style can be recognized only in vessels made after about 1760, despite convincing evidence that the village was making pottery much earlier. Before the mid-eighteenth century, styles were too uniform to distinguish between adjoining villages such as Cochiti–Santo Domingo, Acoma-Laguna, Tesuque–San Ildefonso, and in this case, Zia–Santa Ana.

Around 1760, however, most of the population of Santa Ana moved a few miles east and founded the village of Ranchitos near the Rio Grande, where the reliable availability of water made farming much easier. As a result of the move, Santa Ana potters were farther from a source of black volcanic rock to crush for tempering the clay of their ceramics and closer to an abundance of fine, waterworn sand to use for that purpose. Although Pueblo potters are very reluctant to change their materials, waterworn sand had a legitimacy stemming from a history of use at San Felipe and Isleta. Accordingly the Santa Ana potters made the switch, and since then their work is clearly differentiated from that of Zia, where potters still temper the clay with easily recognized, finely crushed chunks of black rock.

Following the change in tempering material, the styles of the two villages slowly diverged, and the bold red designs seen here appear on most Santa Ana pottery after about 1800. Many traditional pottery elements persisted. In form, this bowl carries echoes of bowls from the early eighteenth century, with a convex underbody and tall concave rim; here, however, the transition in curvature is smooth, in contrast to the earlier, sharply angular transition. Other traditional elements are the red band below the design area and the short gaps in the encircling framing lines. Black pigment had replaced red at the top of the rim around 1800.

Large bowls such as this are traditionally used for mixing bread dough. It is said that the bowl should never be cleaned, so that the spirits of the previous batch of dough can be incorporated into the substance of each successive one.   *Francis H. Harlow*

*Potters from Santa Ana Pueblo
visit the IARC, 1984.*

Jemez Revival Jar

Jemez Pueblo, ca. 1910–20
IAF.545
Height: 25.4cm   Diameter: 26.9cm
Acquired in 1926

Jemez Pueblo has had a long history of pottery making. From the fourteenth century until the Pueblo Revolt in 1680, the village produced vessels that are thoroughly distinct from those of any other pueblo. Characteristic features include the oyster white color, the nature of the design pigment, the designs themselves, and many of the very specialized forms.

But Jemez ceased producing pottery about 1700, relying thereafter on other villages for its vessels. Indeed, some of the finest classic Zia pots of the eighteenth century have been recovered from the back rooms of Jemez dwellings, where they sat for several centuries after being retired from active use. The exchange between Jemez and Zia was especially convenient for both villages. Jemez is situated in a fertile valley, with the Jemez River furnishing abundant water for crops. Zia is about ten miles farther downstream, where the terrain is more parched and harder to farm. Since 1300, Zia potters had been producing excellent vessels of great serviceability, while Jemez farmers and hunters produced food in abundance.

Thus, the circumstances for trade were ideal until the latter years of the nineteenth century, when commercial pans and dishes became easily obtainable and pottery was made for the tourist trade. Around 1900, recognizing the opportunity for a major new money-making industry, Jemez potters began experimenting with a succession of vessels that combined elements of the classic styles of their ancestors with a variety of new ideas. The newly revived craft quickly blossomed into the production of some very handsome vessels.

In this jar we can see the influence of Zia pottery in form, the use of a thick, light-colored slip, and certain design elements—for example, the "eye" at the tip of each crosshatched triangle. Also notable are the short breaks in the encircling framing lines, which continue a tradition that began many centuries earlier. Here, indeed, is a fine example of Pueblo pottery making, never stagnant, always evolving from traditional roots, borrowing the best ideas from neighbors, and continuously responding to changing purposes.
Francis H. Harlow

Jemez Pueblo, ca. 1915.

Acoma Polychrome Water Jar

Acoma Pueblo, ca. 1880–90
IAF.682
Height: 29.2cm   Diameter: 33.0cm
Acquired in 1927

Bird symbolism plays an important role in Pueblo religion, and parrots and other birds painted on Acoma pottery have precontact antecedents in the ceramic traditions of Acoma, Laguna, Zia, Zuni, and Hopi. Often called the Acoma parrot, the tropical macaw seen here is a trademark of Acoma Pueblo pottery.

On this unusual four-colored vessel, the macaw grasps branches and leaves with its talons while it plucks berries with its beak. The designs are painted in red, orange, black, and yellow on a background slip of white kaolin clay. The gracefully painted arc-shaped motifs represent a double rainbow. Floral motifs with additional rainbows appear on the smaller side panels. The macaw's bright feathers are associated with the rainbow and, therefore, with rain.

This fine old Acoma jar was collected by the Indian Arts Fund in the 1920s and can be seen in period photographs of the IAF collection displayed at the Fine Arts Museum in Santa Fe. It was also featured on the cover of Rick Dillingham's *Acoma & Laguna Pottery*. *Michael J. Hering*

Acoma Pueblo potter Lucy Lewis and her daughters at the IARC, 1983. From left: Emma Lewis Mitchell, Dolores Lewis Garcia, Lucy Lewis, Ann Lewis Hansen.

Tesuque Polychrome Storage Jar

Tesuque Pueblo, ca. 1870–80
IAF.843
Height: 40.6cm   Diameter: 48.2cm
Acquired in 1928

The potters of the Tewa villages made vessels in a succession of styles that for centuries were very similar to each other. But early in the nineteenth century, all over the Pueblo Indian world, villages began to develop their own distinctive ceramic signatures. Tesuque, the southernmost Tewa-speaking pueblo, was no exception.

This large storage jar is a magnificent example of Tesuque pottery-making excellence in the late nineteenth century and a veritable catalog of the distinctive design features that make Tesuque pottery easily identifiable. Notice especially the little hooks that embellish the connected diamond-shaped figures on the neck; the six-pointed flower motifs on the body, with short slashes and squiggles in the petals; the four prominent, crosshatched "key" figures sprouting from a circular center, with triple-arc end caps at their extremities; and the horizontal stems with paired leaves.

Design departures from other Tewa pueblos, such as San Ildefonso, do not preclude the strict adherence to many traditional features that have distinguished Tewa pottery since 1600, and in some respects even earlier. The fine, gritty, tan clay, the laboriously stone-polished surfaces of the clay below the red band, the buckskin-colored slip above, the narrow, blood red band below the designs and on the rim top, and the use of plant juice for the black designs are all characteristic features of Tewa pottery.

This jar has been much used for the storage of dry food, perhaps corn or beans, and shows the patina of many hands touching its surfaces. It was obtained in 1928 from Catherine Duran at

Tesuque, who believed that it had been owned by her grandmother. Many other superbly decorated vessels from the same period exhibit a very similar style of design, so that we have not just a distinctive Tesuque signature, but likely also that of a particular individual whose skill and creativity rank among the finest of Pueblo potters. No wonder this jar was so cherished that it received the standard repair treatment of being tied with wet rawhide that would gradually shrink and thereby prevent any cracks from destroying a prized possession. *Francis H. Harlow*

Tesuque Pueblo potter, ca. 1915.

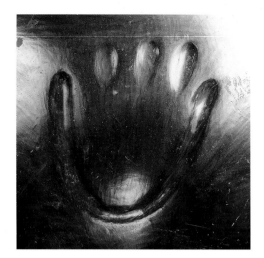

Santa Clara Black Storage Jar

Margaret Tafoya
Santa Clara Pueblo, ca. 1920
IAF.881
Height: 55.9cm Diameter: 53.3cm
Acquired in 1928

Polished black pottery has a long and honored history in Pueblo Indian ceramics. The process originated at least as far back as the twelfth century, when beautifully polished bowls were fired in a brisk, oxidizing fire, then treated while still hot to the chemically reducing action of a strawlike material in the interior. The result was a complete change of the iron oxide in the clay or slip, from an oxygen-rich rust red color to the jet black of an oxygen-poor compound.

In the Tewa pueblos this nearly forgotten process was revived around 1730 to produce a pottery type designated by the Indian name for Santa Clara Pueblo: Kapo Black. Although fine examples of the polished-black style have been produced at most of the Tewa villages, Santa Clara remains its principal home today.

This large storage jar demonstrates the ability of twentieth-century Santa Clara potters to carry on the complex craftsmanship necessary to create such vessels from the earth materials found around the village and to accomplish the delicate firing technique with perfect control. Margaret Tafoya and her family are the most famous of the Santa Clara potters who are able to make such large jars.

The process is long and arduous, extending over many months. The clay must be carefully prepared and tempered to exacting specifications with finely crushed volcanic tuff. To build the jar, coils of clay are curved around, snugged into place, then scraped to essentially the final form. Slow drying is crucial. When the clay has cured, the surface is covered with a fine-textured suspension of rust red slip, then polished with smooth stones that are family heirlooms. The slip-and-polish process may be repeated many times until the surface is perfect.

Firing is a harrowing process that must be done on a windless morning. Slabs of fuel are placed around the jar, which sits on a foundation of rocks. The fire must be carefully tended to control the temperature and ensure the maintenance of an oxygen-poor atmosphere. Months of labor can be lost when the pressure of a residual moisture pocket or impurity fragment results in a tiny explosion that cracks the vessel wall.

This beautiful jar is decorated with a Santa Clara trademark, the bear-paw design. Carved into the clay before the slip was applied, it symbolizes the legend of a bear that led the people to a new spring of water during an unusually dry season. The earliest occurrence of the bear paw on Santa Clara pottery dates to the late nineteenth century. *Francis H. Harlow*

Laguna Polychrome Jar

Laguna Pueblo, ca. 1850
IAF.1026
Height: 48.2cm   Diameter: 63.5cm
Acquired in 1928

This magnificent storage jar illustrates how individual creativity and outside influence play important roles in promoting innovation and change within a pottery tradition. Kenneth Chapman, the first curator of the Indian Arts Fund, collected this piece at Puguate village near Laguna Pueblo in 1928. He purchased it from Locario Chavez, who said a potter named Arroh-ah-och had made it for his grandmother. Locario's father, John Chavez, who was born in 1867, remembered the jar being in his mother's possession when he was a child, and stated that the maker was about sixty years old at the time. Based on this information and a stylistic analysis of the vessel, Chapman dated it to the 1850s. Rick Dillingham, in his *Acoma & Laguna Pottery,* suggested it could date as late as 1900.

Chapman attributed the vessel to Arroh-ah-och, the famous man-woman, or *berdache*, from Laguna Pueblo. In traditional Native American culture the *berdache* is a recognized gender-role reversal and refers to a male who chooses at an early age to dress and live as a woman. In *The Pueblo Potter: A Study of Creative Imagination in Primitive Art,* anthropologist Ruth Bunzel described a specific pot she had seen at Laguna, which Dillingham believed was this very piece. Bunzel reported that Arroh-ah-och had visited Zuni and was so impressed by their ceramics that he introduced the deer motif and other typical Zuni designs into Laguna.

Documented works attributed to Arroh-ah-och can be found in several museum collections. On this pot, the two large Zuni-like medallion designs, the Zuni mule deer with heartline, the phalluses on each animal, and the large hooked scrolls, described by H. P. Mera as the Zuni rain bird motif, are all painted in his distinctive style. The scrolls may also represent feathered prayer sticks, called *pahos,* or the older style of hooked drumsticks with appended feathers in combination with leaf and floral elements. *Michael J. Hering*

San Ildefonso Polychrome Jar

Maria Martinez and Julian Martinez
San Ildefonso Pueblo, 1926
IAF.1166
Height: 39.4cm   Diameter: 48.2cm
Acquired in 1928

Maria and Julian Martinez made several unusual choices in this masterpiece. Maria shaped a unique, nearly ovoid pot, with the upper body sloping gently away from the neck to meet a subtle low shoulder. This shape provided Julian with two large painting surfaces, an upper and a lower, which he used to great advantage, creating a design that should be viewed both from above (see cover) and from the side.

Seen from above, the four solid black triangles that surround the opening and the layout of the design in quadrants pendant from the neck are contrary to traditional San Ildefonso design. They were influenced by the great Hopi-Tewa potter Nampeyo, whose work emulated ancient Hopi wares. San Ildefonso potter Toñita Roybal, sister-in-law of Maria Martinez, began adapting Nampeyo's shapes and designs to her own work around 1920, and this was probably Julian's inspiration. On the underbody is a garland of alternating motifs, including trefoils set in arches, which complement and lend weight to the upper design. In order to suggest symmetry and to imply that the motifs continue around the pot, Julian repeated them six times rather than four. From the side, therefore, the design appears to be symmetrical from only two points.

Julian used decorative elements from several sources, including prehistoric Hopi pottery and historic Acoma pottery, and copied some motifs from the work of Florentino Montoya, the greatest pottery painter of San Ildefonso at the beginning of the twentieth century. The practice of borrowing foreign design systems and motifs was pioneered by Florentino and carried on by Julian and some of his contemporaries through the 1930s, presumably as a tribute to the great masters they admired.

Maria's and Julian's polychrome pottery is not as widely known as their black-on-black ware, but it was the first type of pottery they made, and they continued to make it in small quantities until Julian's death in 1943. As is typical of all of her work, Maria shaped this jar perfectly, with walls of extremely even thickness. Julian finished it superbly, with painting that is precise in the execution of its design and its sureness of hand. *Jonathan Batkin*

Julian and Maria Martinez.

Zuni Polychrome Jar

Zuni Pueblo, ca. 1900
IAF.1372
Height: 25.4cm   Diameter: 31.8cm
Acquired in 1929

This water jar makes an important contribution to our understanding of late-nineteenth- and early-twentieth-century Zuni ceramic history. The vessel was purchased for the Indian Arts Fund from Mary Dissette, who had obtained it at Zuni around 1900 when she was a teacher in the Indian Service. The vessel's base shows no evidence of use, suggesting that the jar was new when Dissette acquired it.

Water jars collected between 1879 and 1885 by the Smithsonian Institution's Bureau of Ethnology differ significantly in shape from the one shown here. Those earlier examples have a clear definition of base-body and body-neck boundaries. Similarly, the decorations painted on this vessel are unlike those in vogue in the early 1880s. Zuni pottery designs recorded in 1924 by Catalina Zuni resemble those on the piece illustrated here, suggesting that the new designs remained in use well into the twentieth century.

Zuni potter Josephine Nahohai, the second recipient of the School of American Research's Katrin H. Lamon Native American Artist Fellowship, selected this water jar as her favorite in the collection. She and two other olla maidens, Eloise Westika and Rose Gasper, "tried on" water jars when they came to Santa Fe to study the collections.

Olla maidens, a twentieth-century Zuni phenomenon, celebrate traditional water-carrying skills at public performances, both within and outside the pueblo, in which they march, sing, and dance while balancing the jars on their heads. In traditional Zuni life, going to the well involved much more than obtaining water. As a central gathering place, the well also provided young men and women with opportunities for courtship. The vessels used to carry water from Zuni's central well to each household would have been highly visible, explaining why Zuni potters lavished more attention on decorating water jars than any other vessel form. *Margaret Ann Hardin*

Zuni Pueblo olla maidens at the IARC, 1985.
From left: Rose Gasper, Josephine Nahohai,
Eloise Westika.

Hano Polychrome Jar

Nampeyo
Hopi First Mesa, ca. 1915–17
IAF.1645
Height: 27.9cm   Diameter: 48.2cm
Acquired in 1931

When Nampeyo coiled clay to shape a jar, she worked as instinctively as all Pueblo potters who have for centuries fashioned vessels for domestic use, ceremonies, and trade. But among Hopi and Hopi-Tewa potters in the early 1900s, only Nampeyo (ca. 1860–1942) became renowned. Her work reflected historic changes in the culture of her people, from the isolation of the Hopi mesas of her youth to the eventual inundation of those mesas by anthropologists, photographers, artists, missionaries, and tourists. Acceding to demand, Nampeyo made jars and bowls for the visitors, interpreting designs and shapes of pottery found in the ancient ruins around her stone village of Hano. By 1900 she had refined her personal style to create vessels of elegance, a style later named Hano Polychrome.

Like potters before her, she did not explain her designs, and contemporary interpretations differ as to the meaning of the anthropomorphic figures on opposite sides of this jar. One elder potter of Nampeyo's family has said that the figure is a rain beetle that comes out before a rain. The circular design, she said, is the sky, and all the design elements within represent the feathers and tails of birds hanging from the sky. A younger potter said that the figure looked like a woman giving birth in a kneeling or squatting position. The circular design, starting with a point in the center, was the road of life through happy events and sad ones, a "calendar" of the child's lifetime, and the vertical designs were clothes, including the woven sashes worn by women.

No doubt each viewer will have his or her own interpretation, but we might ask ourselves how much symbolism matters. Must we interpret beauty? This jar by Nampeyo is a quintessential example of individual creativity that revitalized an indigenous art. *Barbara Kramer*

Hopi potter Nampeyo, ca. 1910.

Zia Polychrome Storage Jar

Isabel Torrebio
Zia Pueblo, ca. 1922
IAF.1668
Height: 43.1cm   Diameter: 53.3cm
Acquired in 1931

Isabel Torrebio began signing her pottery in the early 1920s, a decade before signing became popular at Zia Pueblo. Her painted and fired-in signature appears on another large storage jar that was collected for Merriwether Post in 1922 and eventually donated to the Smithsonian Institution. The vessel illustrated here is identical to the Smithsonian specimen, but was not signed.

A classic example of the continuation of Zia pottery design concepts from earlier times, this vessel is painted with four Zia birds encircled by a large double rainbow. Each of the four design fields includes abstract prayer feathers and rain clouds gathering over mountains. The pot was made with the same kind of brick red clay and crushed black basaltic temper that has been used at Zia for more than five hundred years.

The Pueblo tradition of making large storage jars to hold water, grain, or other foodstuffs dates back many centuries. Those produced at Zia were widely traded to the nearby villages of Jemez, Santa Ana, San Felipe, and Santo Domingo. Massive older jars have been found preserved with some frequency because as storage containers they were regularly in use, quite heavy when filled, and placed in out-of-the-way rooms where they could be protected. In the 1930s Kenneth Chapman and Harry Mera collected a number of late-eighteenth- and nineteenth-century Zia storage jars at Jemez Pueblo. Several had been in constant use for more than one hundred years.

As metal and wooden utilitarian containers of all sizes reached the Pueblo villages in the late nineteenth century, many forms of pottery ceased to be made. But Zia had less contact with the outside world and was less affected by the coming of the railroad than pueblos located closer to towns, and traditional ceramics remained in use there into the 1930s. Zia water jars were used by women to gather water every day from the Jemez River. Women transported the full jars up the mesa on their heads until they reached home and emptied them into a larger storage jar. This centuries-old practice was abandoned in 1928 when a water hydrant was installed in the village. Isabel Torrebio's jar is an outstanding example of the large functional water storage jars produced just before smaller, nonutilitarian pottery became the norm. *Michael J. Hering*

*Potter Elizabeth Medina of Zia Pueblo
at an SAR Open House, 1987.*

Zuni Polychrome Jar

Zuni Pueblo, ca. 1900–1910
IAF.2015
Height: 25.4cm   Diameter: 35.6cm
Acquired in 1936

Harry P. Mera drew heavily on ceramic vessels in the Indian Arts Fund collection when he prepared his classic 1938 publication, *The "Rain Bird": A Study in Pueblo Design*, and he used this water jar as the book's frontispiece. Mera found multiple origins for the rain bird but argued that its presence in the historic period was the result of a revival of precontact black-on-white decorations at Zuni that took place after 1700. Today it is possible to add further details to the framework Mera provided. The reintroduction of earlier decorative elements was a characteristic of nineteenth-century pottery making at Zuni Pueblo. After 1800 Zuni potters experimented with a variety of large, hatched, black-on-white designs, based primarily on precontact pottery found in the immediate area. Among the early-nineteenth-century motifs are two different designs, both recognizable as rain birds. By the late 1870s, the motif that Mera took as his starting point had become a standard form used by a number of potters.

The rain bird on the body of the water jar shown here was the starting point for Mera's derivation of a wide range of motifs. In the design on the neck of the vessel, the rain bird is reduced to the hatched central coil and a few appended elements. The red-hatched design on the neck of IAF.1372 (see page 43) is a similar derivation. In Mera's analysis, small solid designs that incorporate the coiled element constitute a more distant variation. (The little red birds on SAR.1979-6-3 belong to this class of designs; see page 57.)

Zuni potter Milford Nahohai sees in the motif on the water jar's body a representation of rain-bearing clouds rolling into the Zuni valley. As the clouds' leading edges roll under the main mass, they create a curve resembling a bird's beak. *Margaret Ann Hardin*

Puname Polychrome Jar

Zia Pueblo, ca. 1680
IAF.2156
Height: 24.2cm   Diameter: 30.5cm
Acquired in 1941

One of the most significant old Zia pottery vessels in existence, this water jar is the type specimen of Puname Polychrome, a variety that was produced at Zia Pueblo from about 1680 to 1750. It was derived from an earlier type known as Kotyiti Glaze Polychrome, a glaze ware made in the middle Rio Grande valley until the second half of the seventeenth century.

Only twenty-four intact Puname Polychrome pots are known to exist, although an abundance of sherds have been excavated at Zia and five older satellite villages surrounding the present pueblo. Puname sherds have also been found at Jemez Pueblo, the Spanish colonial village of Las Huertas near Placitas, and Gobernador Canyon. The jar illustrated here, like many of the other unbroken vessels, was found in Gobernador Canyon in northwestern New Mexico, far from its village of manufacture.

The populating of the Gobernador area by Pueblo people was directly related to the turmoil and dislocation of the Pueblo Revolt of 1680. Zia people were among the refugees. They took their pottery with them to their new home, where some of them lived until the middle of the eighteenth century. Puname Polychrome shapes and designs are similar to styles of pottery made at Acoma, Zuni, and the Hopi villages during the same period, apparently as a result of the increased contact among the four communities during the Pueblo Revolt.

This Puname jar exemplifies how new ideas were added to earlier motifs from Kotyiti Glaze Polychrome to form the new style. The painted motifs are organized into four equal design panels that repeat themselves in an ABAB pattern. The prominent bilaterally symmetrical bird motif is painted in a vibrant red and is flanked by triangular black-capped feather motifs. Contemporary Zia potters interpret the bird as a bird of prey, possibly an eagle. Directly below the main design panels on the low shoulder are red rainbows. Birds and feathers are associated with prayers for rain, fertility, and new growth. The rainbow is a striking visual phenomenon in the arid Southwest and proof of a successful rainfall. All are apt symbols to decorate a jar made as a container for water, the essence of life.
Michael J. Hering

Michael J. Hering lectures on Zia pottery, 1994.

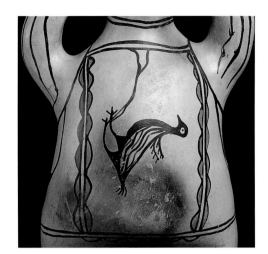

Cochiti Polychrome Figurine
Cochiti Pueblo, ca. 1885–90
IAF.2463
Height: 43.1cm   Width: 20.9cm
Acquired in 1954

Precontact Puebloan cultures produced a great variety of ceramic figurative forms including fetishes, figurines, and effigy vessels. The Spanish clergy destroyed these "primitive idols" and discouraged their manufacture and use. Consequently the historic period saw a marked decline in the production of such forms. For reasons that are not known, however, potters from Cochiti Pueblo began producing large, hollow figurines in abundance around 1875.

Of these, perhaps the most remarkable were standing human figures, like the one shown here, that were made until 1905 and that dealers and collectors disparaged as "grotesques," "monos," or "eccentrics." Many of these curiosities were unquestionably portraits of the white man. The "primitive idols" promoted and marketed by early Santa Fe dealer Jake Gold in fact represented opera singers, carnival and vaudeville figures, cowboys, businessmen, and, as in the case of this figure, priests. The impetus for these humorous imitations was twofold: along with Anglo tourists and assorted professionals, the railroad brought carnivals, circuses, and vaudevilles to New Mexico in the 1880s. In turn, it took Cochiti men to Washington and New York, where they were introduced to the opera, resulting perhaps in the stereotypical operatic poses that their wives reproduced in clay.

With its tonsure, surplice, and crucifix, this figure is obviously a priest, but it is also painted with both abstract and figurative pottery designs, including a large bird on the back. Such a mix of Anglo garb and Cochiti pottery designs, especially those associated with rain and fertility, is the distinctive feature of all these monos. The combination of caricature and sacred symbols is reminiscent of Pueblo ritual clowns imitating white men. This figure is most likely a portrait of a Cochiti clown dressed up as a priest. Such sacred clowns do indeed control rainmaking.

Cochiti female potters could not dress up as white men and mock them on the plaza, but they did what men could not do—they clowned in clay, fixed a fleeting instant of humorous inversion, and enjoyed yet another laugh when they sold such figures to the objects of their satire, who were eager to own a "primitive idol." Native peoples everywhere have responded to invasion and oppression by outsiders by using their traditional arts to strike back in just this way. *Barbara A. Babcock*

Santo Domingo Polychrome Jar

Santo Domingo Pueblo, ca. 1930
IAF.2939
Height: 33.6cm   Diameter: 44.4cm
Acquired in 1963

This handsome jar illustrates a twentieth-century Santo Domingo interpretation of a pottery type called Kiua Polychrome that originated in the late eighteenth century. The lowest of its three design bands features a pattern common on traditional nineteenth-century vessels. The middle and top bands are more modern for Santo Domingo, although their patterns have origins in much earlier vessels of other Pueblo villages. The horizontal arms in the middle band, for example, are reminiscent of motifs used on Tewa Indian pottery a century earlier.

One very traditional feature—carried to an extreme here—is the vertical cleavage of the entire design area by a narrow gap. This break appears on countless pots since at least the thirteenth century, usually as an interruption of framing or path lines. Another traditional feature is the red band below the design area. Seen for centuries on pottery from many of the Rio Grande pueblos, the band was narrow on Tewa vessels and quite wide on those of Santo Domingo and Cochiti. Here the band is very wide, leaving only a narrow unslipped surface near the base. The black rim top became the rule for pots made at Santo Domingo and Cochiti after about 1800, in contrast to Tewa pottery, on which the rim top was painted red until as late as 1915.

The maker created this handsome vessel within the design constraints of the previous century—bold, simple geometrics in vegetal black pigments. Other Santo Domingo potters were more adventurous as they explored ways to capture a part of the expanding market for Native American art. Flowers and birds were executed in black or red with black edging, and during one brief period, virtually the entire vessel surface was covered with large blocks of black and red pigments.

Kiua is the Indian name for Santa Domingo Pueblo. Kiua Polychrome has also been made at nearby Cochiti Pueblo, and sometimes it is not easy to decide which village produced a particular example. Usually the Cochiti variety can be distinguished on the basis of design embellishments that were shunned by Santo Domingo potters. There is no ambiguity about this example, a very typical Santo Domingo product. *Francis H. Harlow*

Santo Domingo Pueblo potters Dolorita Melchor (left)
and Crucita Melchor at the IARC, 1992.

Zuni Polychrome Jar

Tsayutitsa
Zuni Pueblo, ca. 1925
SAR.1979-6-3
Height: 31.8cm   Diameter: 40.6cm
Acquired in 1979

This marvelous water jar is attributed to Tsayutitsa, one of the finest potters to work in the Zuni tradition. She is remembered for her exceptional ability in building very large vessels, and created her pieces in an era in which traditional pottery was being replaced by commercial products in many areas of daily life. Tsayutitsa's water jars, storage jars, and pottery drums were actively acquired by museums and individual collectors, primarily through traders. In 1939, one of her large storage jars, painted with an intricate version of a rain bird design, won a blue ribbon at the Gallup Inter-Tribal Indian Ceremonial.

The designs that decorate this jar became a part of the Zuni tradition in the third quarter of the nineteenth century. By 1850, Zuni potters were using composite designs, with horizontal bands of design punctuated by large medallions, on the bodies of their water jars. Three bands of deer, painted in profile, encircle the body of one water jar collected at Zuni in the early 1870s. By 1879, Zuni potters were painting deer inside arching houses and using them in a variety of water jar decorations. Deer and medallions have remained popular water jar decorations at Zuni throughout the twentieth century.

Tsayutitsa was a creative painter who developed her own distinctive versions of Zuni vessel decorations. Here she employs several strategies to personalize this most recognizable of Zuni patterns. She begins with an unusual variant of the composite design layout. Instead of punctuating the horizontal design fields with two medallions, she repeats her arrangement three times. The medallions themselves are unusually elaborate, each containing three sets of petal outlines rather than the usual one or two. Each set of petals is different. The use of cross-hatching in the innermost petals is also unusual. In the deer house, a distinctive checkered band has been added to the standard parallel lines. This exquisite attention to the smallest details of design is a hallmark of Tsayutitsa's painting. *Margaret Ann Hardin*

Tewa Polychrome Bowl

Astialakwa, ca. 1700
SAR.1983-24-1
Height: 16cm   Diameter: 41cm
Acquired in 1983

In 1680, the Pueblo Indians revolted against their Spanish rulers and drove them south to the vicinity of modern El Paso. Many years of turmoil followed, until Don Diego de Vargas returned with a new flock of Spanish settlers in 1694, initiating decades of uneasy coexistence with the thoroughly demoralized Pueblo populations. Some of the Native villages were abandoned as the residents fled to less accessible sites in the rugged mesas and canyons of the Pajarito Plateau, and even farther to live with the Hopi Indians or with their former enemies, the Navajos, far to the northwest.

This handsome bowl, made by Tewa-speaking Indians during the Revolt years, was a direct witness to this tragic era. Carried along during the heart-wrenching retreat from the ancestral Tewa villages, it found its way to one of the refugee sites along the Jemez River a few miles from the present site of Jemez Pueblo, where it remained for nearly three centuries.

When this bowl was made, styles of Tewa pottery had not become differentiated into the more obvious village styles that emerged in the early nineteenth century, so we cannot be certain where it was produced. In every respect the bowl was true to the canons of its time. The form is especially characteristic. From the rather shallow, rounded underbody, the tall rim is set off by a sharply angular bend that is very typical of Tewa bowls from 1600 to around 1750 and was also popular with neighboring Pueblo villages. On Tewa bowls, including this one, the tall rim is usually slightly concave and bears a design band framed above and below with single lines. Later, with the loss of the angular bend, the single framing lines became pairs. The designs, painted with vegetal juice *(guaco)*, are simple and bold, with solid and hatched triangles and dotted arcs whose significance is today unknown.

The survival of this bowl through both human travail and the weathering of centuries is a tribute to the skill of the potter. The slightly gritty clay and temper were fired to a thoroughly enduring hardness, while the white exterior slip and paint and the red interior slip were so skillfully applied and finished that they look nearly as fresh today as they did at the time the vessel was abandoned. *Francis H. Harlow*

Mojave Ware Effigy Jar

Mojave, ca. 1885
SAR.1994-4-244
Height: 22.25cm
Acquired in 1994

Mojave creation stories tell of the ancient First Times, when the creator Mastamho made, named, and designated the proper function of all important living beings, inanimate things, ceremonies, and geographical features. He led the people to their territory and taught them farming techniques. He gave them agricultural implements, food, and cooking vessels, including scoops, ladles, and bowls, but there is no mention of vessels with handles or human heads among the implements. His work completed, Mastamho transformed into an eagle and flew to the peaks along the Colorado River.

Mojave women were well known along the Colorado River for their ceramics. A potter gathered clay from a private source and worked in a site away from her busy household. She fired utilitarian ceramics in an open pit and worked primarily in the winter, when wood and clay dried completely. If the material proved difficult, or her hands unexpectedly clumsy, the woman said that the clay did not like her that day, and she tried again later. She decorated her own figurines, vessels, and utensils.

Mojave pottery production exploded in the mid-1880s with the coming of the Santa Fe Railroad through Needles, California. Passengers could have lunch and shop in the marketplace, where they bought small figurines and decorative ceramics directly from Mojave potters. Presumably the Mojave produced the more complex ceramic forms to please the tourists. At the railroad station cafeteria and shop, potters saw baskets with handles, breadbaskets, creamers, and pitchers and added these shapes to their repertoire. They probably adopted the small faces and heads from archaeological effigy vessels. The exact derivation of Mojave ceramic forms and details may never be determined because funerary custom demanded that a person's private property be burned during the cremation of his or her body. Almost no early materials, ceramic or otherwise, survived immolation, making it nearly impossible to reconstruct ceramic sequences and changes.

Mojave potters elaborated their wares with great inventiveness. They often crafted multiple spouts, as in this example, fashioned two or three handles, decorated the rims with several effigy heads, and adorned these with beaded necklaces and earrings. They also made effigies of frogs, fish, and owls. Although the forms were often innovations, the painted motifs were usually traditional. This vessel is adorned with the "yellowhammer's belly" design, named for the black-tipped markings on the bird's feathers. *Jill Leslie McKeever Furst*

Mojave woman, Needles, California, ca. 1883.

Mojave Ware Figurine

Mojave, ca. 1880
SAR.1994-4-5
Height: 29.85cm
Acquired in 1994

In precontact times, the Mojaves lived along the Colorado River, from today's Boulder Dam south to Blythe, California. Spanish explorers passed through Mojave territory during and after the late sixteenth century, and the clergy made a few attempts to missionize the people. When the Southwest became part of the United States, the government sponsored a succession of expeditions to explore the length and course of the Colorado and to find the best overland railroad and wagon routes to California.

Travelers noted Mojave clothing, ceramic wares, and farming methods, but did not mention the crafting or use of lively unfired clay figures until the 1880s. If early potters made any prototypes, perhaps these were comparable to images bound into cradleboards by their Quechan (Yuma) neighbors to the south. The Quechan used the little statues in their funeral ceremonies and touched them to the mourners to assure the grief-stricken family that new children would arrive to replace the departed one. There is no specific record of similar practices among the Mojaves, however.

Mojave potters were women. They fashioned simple human features—a head, torso, arms, legs, and genitalia—and added color to the bodies and faces. Red represented temporary body paint, and black represented permanent tattoos. The Mojaves changed their painted patterns as often as they could, and wealthier people redrew or refreshed the motifs on their bodies every day. Some patterns were confined to men and others to women, but the most common one, drawn on both male and female figurines, consisted of red vertical stripes on the torsos, sometimes over a coating of white or yellow pigment.

This typical figurine wears a motif called *hotahpam*, or bridle, for its resemblance to a horse's bridle. It consists of an hourglass shape on each cheek. The black lines down the chin represent one of the most common women's tattoo patterns. The figurine wears only a beaded necklace and earrings and a wraparound skirt held at the waist by a string belt. Her creator tore the cloth into strips to simulate shredded bark, the traditional material of male and female garments. The little figure is barefoot, and often the potters enlarged the feet to enable the figures to stand. The treatment of the hair differentiates Mojave from neighboring Quechan figures. The Mojave glued the hair onto the top of the head, often over a painted black cap. The Quechan formed a deep hole, tied the hair into a single swatch, and inserted the bound end into the depression; then they added a headband that formed a roll around the crown.

This figurine was part of a major bequest of Mojave artifacts from Rick Dillingham.
Jill Leslie McKeever Furst

Mojave figurines from the Rick Dillingham Collection.

Cochiti Polychrome Storyteller

Helen Cordero
Cochiti Pueblo, mid-1960s
SAR.1994-5-60
Height: 26.8cm   Length: 20.4cm
Acquired in 1994

Helen Cordero of Cochiti Pueblo first tried her hand at pottery making in the late 1950s under the tutelage of her kinswoman, Juanita Arquero. She soon discovered that she was far more adept at making figurines, for which Cochiti had long been famous, than she was at shaping bowls and jars. The first time she "showed out" her "little people" at a Santo Domingo feast day, architect and folk art collector Alexander Girard purchased all she had and encouraged her to make more and larger figures. After he bought a singing mother, or "madonna," figure, Girard asked Cordero to make a larger figure with more children. Thus, the first "storyteller" was produced in 1964.

The distinctive figures began winning prizes immediately and quickly became popular collector's items. The success of the storyteller initiated a revolution in figurative ceramics, first at Cochiti and later at other Pueblo villages. Cordero's storytellers led to a large repertoire of figurative forms, including nativities, drummers, singing mothers, nightcriers, mother owls, and turtles carrying children on their backs, but the storyteller remained her personal favorite as well as the most popular among her patrons. Over the years the figure became more refined and more complicated, sanded ever more smoothly and covered with so many layers of white slip that his surface—sometimes covered with as many as thirty appliquéd children—was pearlescent.

This male figure with five children, like all Cordero's storytellers, is a portrait of her grandfather, Santiago Quintana. He was a famous and gifted storyteller who recited stories not only to his own grandchildren and great-grandchildren but also to several generations of anthropologists, from Adolph Bandelier to Ruth Benedict. Compared to storytellers from the mid-1970s, this one is simpler in design and rounder in its proportions. The painted surface combines Pueblo and Christian iconography, Pueblo pottery designs, and Pueblo and Anglo textile designs, a melange that recalls the unusual bicultural painted garb of nineteenth-century Cochiti figurines. The closed eyes on this storyteller, a feature developed in collaboration with Sallie Wagner in the mid-1960s, became Cordero's trademark. *Barbara A. Babcock*

Helen Cordero, ca. 1983.

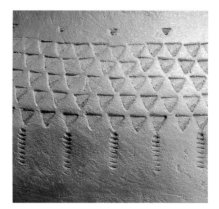

Micaceous Jar

Ramita Martinez and Juan José Martinez
Picuris Pueblo, ca. 1960
SAR.1994-5-70
Height: 22.8cm   Diameter: 24.2cm
Acquired in 1994

Micaceous pottery was the last Southwestern Indian ceramic tradition to make the transition from utility and cooking wares to varied forms of art pottery and sculpture. Unlike potters working in other painted and blackware traditions, who were heavily influenced by anthropologists, micaceous pottery makers made the change in the 1990s, largely without outside influence.

In the 1860s simple bowls and jars were the most common form of micaceous pottery, some of which featured "piecrust" rim decorations and occasional "rope fillet" designs on the neck or shoulder. Most of these vessels were shaped using a corncob as a scraper, leaving a brushed and often unslipped surface. One hundred years later, potters were developing new designs and surface treatments as a means of making their wares more attractive to potential buyers who visited the pueblos.

The vessel shown here was made by Ramita Martinez and decorated by her husband, Juan José Martinez, and is an outstanding example of the kind of experimentation that was taking place at Picuris Pueblo in the 1960s. A gift from Sallie Wagner, it features a traditional shape with a piecrust design on the outflaring rim. Juan José's tools included broken triangular files, a beer-bottle opener, and a variety of nails, bolts, and screw eyes, some of which were pounded into squares and diamond shapes. The pattern of triangles on the shoulder was made with a broken file, with pendant designs produced by pressing a stove bolt on edge into the moist clay. Evidence of the corncob-brushed surface can be seen at the neck. The dark fireclouds on the rim enhance the deep golden color produced by the characteristic slip used by Picuris potters. This particular decorative style is unique to the work of Ramita and Juan José Martinez. *Duane Anderson*

Micaceous Art Pottery Vessel

Lonnie Vigil
Nambé Pueblo, 1995
SAR.1995-13-1
Height: 65cm   Diameter: 72cm
Acquired in 1995

Lonnie Vigil of Nambé Pueblo won two awards at the 1995 Santa Fe Indian Market for this twenty-five-gallon micaceous clay vessel fired in the black phase (reducing atmosphere). One was for Large Pottery/Best Traditional Technique; the other was a Second Place/74th Annual Santa Fe Indian Market Award. Four Indian Arts Fund patrons—Sudye and Jim Kirkpatrick and Betty and Luke Vortman—joined forces and purchased this piece for the Indian Arts Research Center. It was a most welcome addition, not so much because it was a ribbon winner but because it so perfectly exemplifies the story of "legacy in the making."

Lonnie Vigil learned to make pottery after leaving a career with the Bureau of Indian Affairs in Washington, D.C. Unsure of his direction, he came home to Nambé Pueblo, roamed the countryside, and prayed. He found a clay source on Nambé tribal lands and later discovered polishing pebbles in the ruins of his grandparents' home. In a cooperative effort between himself and Mother Clay, Vigil began making pottery.

Once he established himself as a potter, Vigil became a key figure in the transformation of micaceous utilitarian wares to a form of art pottery now accorded the same level of aesthetic appreciation as the celebrated painted wares and polished black and red wares of the American Southwest. This transformation can be traced back to 1992, when one of Vigil's gold-phase rainbow jars was named Best of Division at the Santa Fe Indian Market and attitudes about micaceous pottery were changed forever.

In 1994 Vigil became the first Ron and Susan Dubin Native American Artist Fellow at the School of American Research. During his tenure he helped organize and facilitate the first of the School's Native American Artists Convocations. Subsequently Vigil and his colleagues at the convocation organized the first Micaceous Pottery Market in Santa Fe, with more than fifty micaceous potters from the northern Rio Grande region participating.

The high level of technical excellence exhibited in this piece is remarkable, especially considering that it was made on Vigil's kitchen table and fired in the open in his backyard. According to British impressionist painter Bernard Cohen, "this vessel is best thought of as a piece of sculpture. It explores symmetry and simplicity on a grand and delicate scale rarely seen in the ceramic arts." *Duane Anderson*

Lonnie Vigil, 1993.

"Zia Deer Dance." Painting by Velino Shije Herrera, ca. 1926–30.

PAINTINGS

"Buffalo Dancers"
Crescencio Martinez (Ta'e)
San Ildefonso Pueblo
Pencil and watercolor on paper, 1918
IAF.P19
Height: 58.4cm Width: 37.5cm
Acquired in 1918

Crescencio Martinez's reputation as the virtual creator of the modern Pueblo Indian watercolor painting tradition rests on approximately thirty paintings made during the last eighteen months of his life. Most of those works, which so profoundly affected the course of twentieth-century American Indian painting, belong to the School of American Research.

Pueblo painting was a cross-cultural art invented to represent aspects of the artists' world for the use of people from a vastly different "other." This superb example of the period is a characteristic synthesis of the opposing visual concepts that defined the dominant Pueblo and Euro-American artistic traditions of Martinez's time. As in Pueblo art, illusions of depth are minimized, all action is parallel to the picture plane, and each figure is isolated in a spatial void. As in Euro-American figurative art, each figure is a convincing, three-dimensional illusion on a two-dimensional surface. Skillful draftsmanship and intelligent brushwork create shadows, mass, and musculature. The tensions that result from harmonizing such different ways of visualizing experience create a compellingly vital expression of complex interactions between two societies.

Those interactions began about 1908, when Martinez and others from San Ildefonso were hired by the School of American Research (then the School of American Archaeology) to help excavate the ruins of their ancestral homes on the Pajarito Plateau. There Martinez became known to and respected by many Anglo scientists and artists. Some became his patrons, among them Edgar L. Hewett, director of the School. The Buffalo Dance was an especially suitable subject for Martinez. Performed annually on San Ildefonso's Feast Day (January 23), it would have been familiar to many in Santa Fe's Euro-American community who were potential art patrons and active defenders of Pueblo political rights, then under extreme threat. This painting was collected by the poet Alice Corbin Henderson, a driving force of the Santa Fe art colony after 1916 and a founding member of the Indian Arts Fund. It was given to the Indian Arts Fund by her friend, novelist and poet Mary Austin. Both women were Indian rights activists who also worked together to promote Indian watercolor painting.

Crescencio Martinez was an uncle of Alfonso Roybal (Awa Tsireh), who later became a key figure in the development of Pueblo painting. Awa Tsireh helped Martinez with his last paintings, made just before his death in June 1918 during a devastating influenza epidemic.
J. J. Brody

Crescencio Martinez, his wife, Maximiliana, and musician and composer Charles Wakefield Cadman, ca. 1915.

"Preparing for the (Hopi) Buffalo Dance"

Otis Polelonema
Hopi
Watercolor on paper, ca. 1920–21
IAF.P44
Height: 28.7cm Width: 36.1cm
Acquired in 1933

With Fred Kabotie and Velino Shije Herrera, Otis Polelonema was one of seven students recruited at the Santa Fe Indian School in 1918 by Elizabeth DeHuff, wife of the school's superintendent, to paint pictures of Pueblo ritual dances at her home. The project only lasted a few months, but in 1919 DeHuff arranged with Edgar L. Hewett to show the young artists' work at the Museum of New Mexico. Polelonema occasionally joined Kabotie, Herrera, and Awa Tsireh as an artist working for the School of American Research at the Palace of the Governors in 1920 and 1921.

Polelonema and Kabotie had been taken to the Santa Fe Indian School from their remote Hopi homes in 1915, and neither one had the opportunity to visit Hopi again until the early 1920s. Kabotie lived in Santa Fe periodically after that, but Polelonema chose to remain at Hopi and to make his life as a farmer in the community where he was born. Nonetheless he continued to paint pictures on paper, always creative, always expressive, filling commissions for patrons or selling pictures at nearby trading posts. He was particularly active and inventive as an artist during the last few years of his life.

During their Santa Fe years, Polelonema and Kabotie were close companions who shared memories of home and painted similar, sometimes identical, Hopi subjects. This is one such picture, probably painted in 1920 and purchased by Alice Corbin Henderson for her friend, Mary Austin. Austin in turn willed it to the Indian Arts Fund. Fred Kabotie made two similar paintings at about the same time, both of them also in the School of American Research collection.

In its illustrative realism and precise detail, the painting is typical of almost everything done by Polelonema, Kabotie, and Herrera during their early years. But the intense, subjective qualities seen here are uniquely characteristic of Polelonema. His interest clearly is in telling about the two men, who are shown preparing costumes and other paraphernalia for a ritual dance. He includes many realistic background details that are instructive about an unfamiliar lifeway, but by bringing us close to the men, he underlines the emotional intensity of their haunting, large-eyed, long-nosed faces. These are pleasant people who appear to be at peace with their work.

In other paintings of this period, Polelonema's people can be infinitely sad and introspective. The awkwardness evident here disappeared as Polelonema matured, but he never lost the sincerity and intensity of his expression. *J. J. Brody*

Otis Polelonema at Hopi, 1959.

Otis Polclonema.

"Two Dancers and a Drummer"

Fred Kabotie (Naqavoy'ma)
Hopi
Gouache on paper, ca. 1928–32
IAF.P93
Height: 30.5cm Width: 24.2cm
Acquired in 1934

Fred Kabotie spent much of the middle and late 1920s in the Santa Fe area working on painting commissions for individuals and museums. This picture seems to date from that period. It was once owned by Mary Cabot Wheelwright, a collector of ritual art and student of non-Western religions, who gave it to the Indian Arts Fund in 1934. In it, Kabotie demonstrates his command of objective Euro-American illustrative traditions, which he uses with expressive effect. The three figures move toward the viewer with massive dignity, walking through a spatial void that is given dimension by their solid presence. Kabotie's style of illusionism is certainly his own invention, but it has precedents at Hopi, where Euro-American professional artists left their traces as early as 1904.

Kabotie first came to Santa Fe in 1915 as a reluctant boarding-school student at the Santa Fe Indian School. He was one of the group recruited by Elizabeth DeHuff to paint at her house, and his work was shown at the 1919 Museum of New Mexico show she arranged. This was the first recorded exhibition of Pueblo watercolor paintings and was well received by the Santa Fe intellectual community. In 1920, the pictures were shown in New York City along with works by Crescencio Martinez and other, older San Ildefonso and Taos Pueblo artists. Indian watercolor painting was suddenly recognized as a "fine art," and young Fred Kabotie became famous as one of its inventors.

The Indian School artists' paintings were more complex and illusionistic than those of Martinez and the older San Ildefonso artists. As the young artists exhibited their work and became famous, their influence grew. In 1920, Hewett hired Kabotie, Herrera, and Awa Tsireh to paint for the School of American Research at the Palace of the Governors. As a result of the interactions among those artists during the next few years, each of them mastered technical skills and expanded his range of expression as, collectively, they created a new Pueblo art.

Within a year or two after making this painting, Kabotie returned to Hopi to teach art. There he profoundly influenced generations of younger Hopi painters. *J. J. Brody*

From left: Unknown, Fred Kabotie, Velino Shije Herrera, probably at the Santa Fe Indian School, ca. 1925.

Fred Kabotie

"Hunting Bison on Horseback"
Velino Shije Herrera (Ma-Pe-Wi)
Zia Pueblo
Gouache on board, ca. 1930
IAF.P114
Height: 73.7cm Width: 50.8cm
Acquired in 1937

This fantasy is a powerful example of one of several modes mastered by Ma-Pe-Wi, who signed his work "Velino Shije" until about 1926. In it he combines a realistically painted narrative scene with stylized symbols arranged in a kind of stage setting. The composition is framed by an elaborate abstract sky and an equally abstract landscape. This painting was collected by Mary Cabot Wheelwright and given by her to the Indian Arts Fund.

Ma-Pe-Wi used opaque colors when painting in this manner, differentiating between the narrative figures that were realistically modeled with light and shade and the abstract ones that were painted flatly. His subject matter also harmonizes oppositions: the framing motifs recall the conventions of Pueblo ritual art, while the romanticized buffalo chase suggests contemporaneous Pan-Indian and Plains Indian art. Despite the obvious differences between his work and that of Crescencio Martinez, their pictorial goals were the same: to harmonize the spatial abstractions of traditional Pueblo art with the illusionistic realism of Euro-American painting.

When this piece was painted, Ma-Pe-Wi was probably familiar with the work of the group of Oklahoma Indian artists known as the Kiowa Five, which was introduced to the Santa Fe area in about 1929. Their stencil-like paintings were also romantic, nostalgic, and made with deep, flatly applied, opaque colors. Their work, like that of Ma-Pe-Wi, clearly predicts the future of Indian painting. Within a decade a similar, Pan-Indian style of watercolor painting would be taught at Indian schools across the nation. Ma-Pe-Wi had great influence on younger painters such as his nephew, Jose Rey Toledo, because of his own achievements and, after about 1936, his work as an art teacher at the Albuquerque Indian School.

Ma-Pe-Wi was an artist for most of his adult life, often living in Santa Fe. As a youngster at the Santa Fe Indian School in 1918 he was the most venturesome artist of the group that painted pictures for Elizabeth DeHuff. His work was included in every important Pueblo painting and Indian art exhibition held in his lifetime, and from 1920 to 1924 he worked closely and productively with Fred Kabotie and Awa Tsireh at Santa Fe's Palace of the Governors. He matured rapidly during those years, and the three young painters became the most influential Pueblo artists of their time. *J. J. Brody*

"Corn Dance"

Alfonso Roybal (Awa Tsireh)
San Ildefonso Pueblo
Watercolor on paper, ca. 1922–23
IAF.P228
Height: 86.4cm Width 57.2cm
Acquired in 1949

This painting dates from the period when Awa Tsireh worked with Fred Kabotie and Ma-Pe-Wi at the Palace of the Governors, making watercolor pictures of Pueblo subjects, especially ritual dances. Their work was supervised by artist, scholar, and museum curator Kenneth Chapman.

Awa Tsireh had initially worked closely with his uncle, Crescencio Martinez, but was now inventing a new way of painting. Having observed and absorbed some of the ambitious pictorial innovations of his young colleagues, he here organizes a far more complex composition than any done earlier by either Crescencio or himself into a stately arabesque structured by crossing diagonals. His figures are stylized, active, robust, and far less illusionistic than in his or his uncle's previous work.

The complexity of this composition owes much to Kabotie and Ma-Pe-Wi, both of whom, from the very first, used diagonals and vanishing-point perspective to create deep spatial illusions. But Awa Tsireh's concern is not so much a matter of visual illusion as a desire to express the patterns of a ritual event, the summer Corn Dance. To that end, he avoids illusionistic conventions in favor of creating a shallow, abstract space. His interest in abstraction, shallow space, and decorative patterning was shared by other early watercolor artists from San Ildefonso Pueblo. It was also a powerful visual and ideological link connecting them to the many Santa Fe intellectuals who were associated in some manner with modernist art movements. Imagist poet Alice Corbin Henderson and her husband, artist William Penhallow Henderson, were Awa Tsireh's first significant patrons and introduced him to the abstract art traditions of the Near and Far East.

Artist John Sloan and collector Elizabeth White also promoted Awa Tsireh's work. White probably owned this painting around the time she opened what may have been the world's first Indian art gallery in New York in 1922. She and Sloan included it when they organized the first national American Indian art exhibition, the Exposition of Indian Tribal Arts, in 1931, and showed it the following year at the Venice Biennale. In 1949, White gave the painting to the Indian Arts Fund, which she had helped to create. *J. J. Brody*

Awa Tsireh, ca. 1929.

"Koshare Climbing Pole"

Abel Sanchez (Oqwa Pi)
San Ildefonso Pueblo
Watercolor on paper, ca. 1925–30
IAF.P236
Height: 59.4cm Width: 41.2cm
Acquired in 1961

Oqwa Pi developed several styles of representational painting that share similar visual qualities: the abstract patterning of bright colors that were usually flatly applied, draftsmanship that was relatively bold and simplified, and frontal pictorial organizations that projected very shallow picture spaces. His boldest, most abstract, and most compelling paintings, such as this one, are simultaneously decorative and expressive. Showing just enough detail for the subject to be identifiable, the painting is about mood rather than instruction. It looks at the light side of the sacred clowns, liminal and dangerous beings portrayed here as more humorous and benign than threatening.

This style of painting by Oqwa Pi was unique in the Pueblo art of the time, and the artist demonstrated extraordinary and apparently fortuitous parallels to the modernist art of the era. Not surprisingly, he was a favorite among those Santa Fe intellectuals who were sympathetic to modernism in art. Possibly for the same reason, he was virtually ignored by those who preferred a more illusionistic art. Elizabeth White sold his paintings in New York but kept many, including this one, in her personal collection. It was part of the 1931–33 Exposition of Indian Tribal Arts.

Oqwa Pi was a slightly younger contemporary of Awa Tsireh. Both attended the San Ildefonso Day School, where their teacher, Esther Hoyt, introduced them to watercolor painting. Nothing is known of Oqwa Pi's art until about 1919, when Alice Corbin Henderson acquired one of his paintings for her friend Mary Austin. That picture most likely was painted after the 1919 exhibition of Pueblo Indian paintings at the Museum of New Mexico. Awa Tsireh saw that exhibition, and Oqwa Pi probably did as well.

Oqwa Pi painted sporadically all his life and was ever inventive. Like many Pueblo artists of his generation, he lived at his pueblo and considered himself to be both farmer and artist. Throughout his adult life he was an honored spiritual and political leader at San Ildefonso.

J. J. Brody

Oqwa Pi in Thunder costume, Palace of the Governors, Santa Fe, 1919.

"Shaking Pollen from the Corn"

Narcisco Abeyta (Ha So De)
Navajo
Gouache on paper, ca. 1938—40
IAF.P312
Height: 35.6cm Width: 30.5cm
Acquired in 1971

Narcisco Abeyta was among the first students in the painting classes known as "The Studio," taught by Dorothy Dunn at the Santa Fe Indian School from 1932 to 1937. Dunn encouraged her students, who came from many different tribes, to base their art on tribal life and the traditions of their own group. Under her guidance, Abeyta developed a unique and expressive approach to picture making. Navajo lifeways and activities were his characteristic subjects then and for the better part of his long artistic career. He often emphasized, as he does here, family-based endeavors such as farming or harvesting wild foods. He also illustrated legendary events, usually showing them as taking place in the same environment and involving the same kinds of people portrayed in his genre scenes.

Most of Abeyta's Navajo contemporaries pictured scenes of Navajo life in more panoramic, illustrative, and objective ways then he did, and they usually represented legendary events as though belonging to a different time, space, and locale. Many created highly imaginary, dramatic, and nostalgic scenes to illustrate a pre-reservation, pre-European past. Younger artists soon began to use a limited number of stock pictorial conventions such as stylized plants, birds, rainbows, and clouds to symbolize time, place, event, and, above all, "Indianness."

Abeyta, however, developed an expressive, bold style of drawing with opaque paint that allowed him to become by far the most "painterly" artist of his generation of Indian School students. Though his work differed so radically from that of most of his contemporaries and soon drifted away from Dunn's ideals, to her credit she encouraged his development. His essentially modernist approach was compatible with such popular and contemporaneous mainstream artists as Raul Dufy and Henri Matisse and bears comparison with the work of Abel Sanchez of San Ildefonso Pueblo.

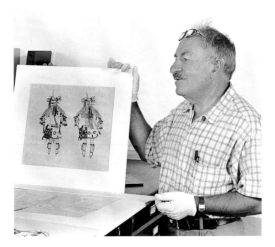

Abeyta studied art at the University of New Mexico after World War II with pioneer modernist Raymond Jonson and abstract expressionist Lez Haas. Subsequently there were long periods when he seems to have painted rarely, intermixed with bursts of creative activity during which he proved himself one of the most inventive Indian artists of the twentieth century. *J. J. Brody*

J. J. Brody lectures at the IARC, 1992.

"Mystical Design: Fertilization of Maize"

Waldo Mootzka
Hopi
Ink and watercolor on watercolor paper, ca. 1937–40
IAF.P313
Height: 55.2cm Width: 38.1cm
Acquired in 1971

Waldo Mootzka was a skilled artist who ordinarily painted in a variation of the illustrative realism made popular among Hopi artists by Fred Kabotie and Otis Polelonema. During the 1930s, however, while working in Santa Fe and not long before his death in an automobile accident, Mootzka painted several remarkable Art Deco–style pictures similar to this one. Using translucent, highly chromatic paints and pen and ink, he harmonized the decorative, modernist stylizations of Art Deco with an idiosyncratic mix of motifs referring to both the Art Deco movement and traditional Hopi beliefs. The motifs—arcs, bubblelike clouds, twining vinelike forms, and stiffly posed, elegant human figures—are all somehow appropriate to the mystical subject matter.

The didactic qualities of modern Hopi illustrative painting were stated explicitly by Fred Kabotie. He intended his art to inform his Euro-American friends and patrons about Hopi lifeways. The ultimate purpose was to promote better and more meaningful interactions between the two groups by explaining aspects of Hopi ideological expression that could legitimately be shared.

Similar goals seem to have inspired Mootzka in his few modernist paintings. Here, imaginatively, even fantastically, he restates in a new idiom some of the visual and ideological themes commonly found in much of the realistic Hopi art of the twentieth century: visual rhythms that simulate the rhythms of ritual events, bilateral symmetry, symbolic use of color, esoteric ritual, corn, clouds, falling rain, lightning, and, most especially, the fusion of oppositions such as female and male principles.

At one time this painting was one of many by early-twentieth-century Pueblo Indian artists that decorated the rooms and lobbies of La Fonda, the Fred Harvey Company's showcase hotel in Santa Fe. In 1940 it was in the collection of Herbert J. Spinden, a pioneer Southwestern anthropologist whose association with the School of American Research dated back almost to its beginnings. Spinden was an early collector of modern Pueblo Indian paintings and, from his base at the Brooklyn Museum, became a major figure in the New York museum world. This painting was one of several that he loaned to the Museum of Modern Art for its trailblazing 1941 exhibition, Indian Art of the United States. *J. J. Brody*

Paper conservator Patricia Morris at the IARC, 1983.

"Eagle Dance"

Tonita Peña (Quah-Ah)
San Ildefonso/Cochiti
Pencil and watercolor on paper, ca. 1925–30
SAR.1978-1-285
Height: 32cm Width: 48cm
Acquired in 1978

Tonita Peña, the first woman to sell her watercolor paintings in the new tradition of Pueblo art, began painting as a child at the San Ildefonso Day School. After graduation in 1906, Peña, newly orphaned, moved to Cochiti Pueblo to live with her aunt and uncle, potter Martina Vigil and pottery painter Florentino Montoya. Under their tutelage she became a potter and pottery painter. Her earliest known paintings on paper date from about 1920 when, as a twice-widowed mother of three young children, she sold paintings to Edgar Lee Hewett. She subsequently became a role model for young Pueblo women painters, and her son, Joe Herrera, became one of the most influential Pueblo artists of his time.

Peña had introduced herself to Hewett as a person who could paint pictures like those in the 1919 Museum of New Mexico exhibition of Pueblo paintings. Hewett sponsored her over the next several years, assigning Kenneth Chapman and other School of American Research staff members the responsibility of supplying her with materials and critical advice. Hewett bought her sometimes-awkward first pictures, often for resale, and as her skills developed, her audience expanded. By 1925 Elizabeth White was a major supporter and promoter of her work, buying Peña's pictures for herself and for sale at her New York Indian art gallery.

White exhibited this painting in the 1931 Exposition of Indian Tribal Art in New York. It remained in her collection and at her death was willed to the Indian Arts Fund. It is a particularly fine example of Peña's early mature work, when she delighted in using bright, crisp colors to delineate detailed patterns of costume. Her forward-leaning figures seem to float in space with a controlled vitality that suggests the rhythms of the pictured dance. Like Awa Tsireh and Oqwa Pi, Peña modified the illustrative realism and deep space of the Indian School artists by her shallow treatment of pictorial space. Those abstract, decorative qualities of color and space belong to a style of painting that came to be associated with early San Ildefonso Pueblo watercolor artists. *J. J. Brody*

Tonita Peña, ca. 1935.

Quah. Ah.

Tonita Peña.

"Gallup Ceremonial Parade"

Jimmy Toddy (Beatien Yazz)
Navajo
Gouache on illustration board, ca. 1946
SAR.1985-7-1
Height: 56cm Width: 71cm
Acquired in 1985

At the time this picture was painted, the teenaged Jimmy Toddy had only recently returned to civilian life after serving with the Marines in China during World War II. Born and raised on the Navajo Reservation near Wide Ruins, Arizona, he was far more knowledgeable about the expressive potentials of painting than most Indian artists of his generation. As a child, Toddy was immersed in a local genre tradition of Navajo art through some relatives who painted for their own pleasure. His passion for art was encouraged by Sallie (Wagner) and William Lippincott, who bought the Wide Ruins trading post in 1938. Among the Lippincotts' visitors were artists and writers who came to experience the novelty of the Navajo Reservation. Young Jimmy Toddy, nicknamed Beatien Yazz (Little No-Shirt), got to know and work with some of these artists and even visited one of them in Chicago for a few weeks. Something of a prodigy, he had his first art exhibit in 1942 and was the subject of a biography in 1944.

In the 1940s and 1950s it was uncommon for Indian artists to paint realistic pictures of urban scenes or to use subjects of contemporary social significance. The Indian schools and the curio market alike encouraged nostalgic, romanticized subjects confined to a limited canon of "Indian" pictorial conventions.

Unconventional in every respect, Toddy's painting was more than two decades ahead of its time. This panoramic street scene illustrates the major annual public event at Gallup, New Mexico. Until the 1950s, the huge Navajo Reservation was relatively isolated, its people largely dependent on the trading posts for manufactured goods and contact with the outside world. The Gallup Ceremonial was designed to attract tourists arriving by the Santa Fe Railroad or by automobile on Route 66, a two-lane highway. Indian people and their exotic ethnic trappings were the attractions, and the event was controlled by local and regional business interests, especially Indian traders and curio dealers. By simply and realistically picturing the parade through Gallup that opens the event, Toddy lays bare some of the fundamental inequalities that characterized relationships between Indians and non-Indians in that time and place.

Sallie Wagner collected hundreds of Jimmy Toddy's pictures, including this one. She gave her collection to the Indian Arts Research Center in the 1980s. *J. J. Brody*

Beatien Yazz, 1982.

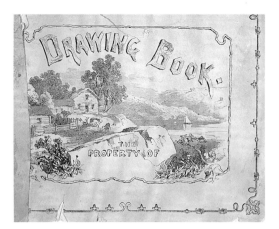

"A Kiowa War Chief"
Charley Ohettoint or his brother Silverhorn (Huangooah)
Kiowa
Pencil, pen, ink, and watercolor on paper in a bound book, ca. 1880
SAR.1990-19-8
Height: 24.2cm Width: 18.5cm
Acquired in 1990

Among the roots of twentieth-century Native American painting are nineteenth-century works on paper made by Plains Indian warriors. It had long been customary for warriors to portray their exploits in historically accurate paintings on animal hides. After about 1850, as ledger books and other sources of paper became available, similar paintings were made as picture books to supplement or replace hide paintings. By then, aboriginal modes of drawing were being modified by Euro-American realistic conventions.

After 1876, warrior-artists from various tribes, including Kiowas who were imprisoned at Fort Marion, Florida, introduced new subjects and stylistic innovations in their work. Paintings of warlike exploits were generally replaced by pictures recording the artists' recent experiences or by nostalgic records of earlier events in the lives of their people. These were often sold for pocket money to wealthy vacationers from the Northeast.

This painting is from a bound book in which a sequence of pictures record in detail Kiowa war, political, and ritual leaders shortly after their resettlement on a reservation in Oklahoma. The "chief" shown here has not been identified, but the heraldic design on the painted teepee is still in use and is the property of an important Kiowa fraternity. More than one artist may have worked on the book, and this picture was probably made by either of two brothers, both former warriors. Silverhorn, the younger of the two, became famous as an assistant to turn-of-the-century anthropologists and for his paintings of pre-reservation Kiowa life. Charley Ohettoint, the older brother, became an educator and agent of change among Kiowa people during the difficult early years of the twentieth century. The two helped ease the transition from the pre- to the post-reservation era. Their artistic legacy extended to the early-twentieth-century group of artists known as the Kiowa Five, who had a strong impact on the development of Indian painting in the 1930s and 1940s.

The book of drawings was presented by Kiowa leaders to Carl Schurz, Secretary of the Interior, during his official visit to the Kiowa Reservation around 1880 and may have been made for that purpose. Schurz's aide Edwin P. Hanna later acquired this drawing; in 1990 his grandson, David Hanna Fairbanks, gave it to the IARC. *J. J. Brody*

Cover of Kiowa ledger book.

A Camp, one Indian was stand at the
door, he was chief,

TEXTILES

Classic Blanket

Navajo, 1850–60
IAF.T8
Length: 165cm Width: 129.5cm
Acquired in 1927

Navajo blankets of the Classic period (1650–1865) are rare today, particularly those with red backgrounds. Red dyes as deep and rich as this were not obtainable from native plants, which tend to produce shades of yellow, beige, and green. Weavers were therefore faced with the long, tedious process of picking apart manufactured red cloth, called baize or bayeta, and re-spinning the crimped threads into yarn. The U.S. Army supplied such cloth by the yard to be made into garments or used for trim. Red seems to have been the most popular color, although green and yellow were also issued.

The dark bars on the ground of this blanket make it appear that the overall grid pattern is laid over or superimposed. This type of net or reticulated design is common in weavings of the Classic period and especially characteristic of the 1850s and 1860s. Initially Navajo textiles were made into dresses, saddle blankets, or, as in this case, outer wearing blankets or "overcoats." Only later, when the Navajos had adopted a settled lifestyle on reservation lands

and traders supplied them with cloth and Pendleton blankets, did they begin making rugs for Anglo homes. Navajo weavers had always made textiles for trade as well as items for their own use. Their blankets were popular with other tribes such as the Ute, Sioux, and Cheyenne, and the weaving skills of Navajo women were highly valued by the Spanish settlers.
Marian Rodee

Marian Rodee lectures on Navajo weaving at the IARC, 1990.

Chief White Antelope Blanket

Navajo, ca. 1860
IAF.T43
Length: 193cm   Width: 142cm
Acquired in 1929

No artifact in the SAR collection better represents the "legacy" theme of this book than the Chief White Antelope blanket. The single most important cultural icon of the Southern Cheyenne tribe, it is believed to have been taken from the body of Chief White Antelope at the Sand Creek Massacre in Colorado on November 29, 1864. Its significance to the Cheyenne people is paralleled by its artistic and art historical significance to the people of the world, for it is generally regarded as the finest example of Navajo weaving created during the Classic period.

Some scholars speculate that the piece was a "slave blanket" made by a Navajo woman who lived, forcibly or otherwise, in a Spanish household. This would help explain the fineness of the work, which was probably done around the time when the Army was conducting its forced removal of the Navajos to Fort Sumner, New Mexico. Some contemporary Cheyenne elders and descendants of Chief White Antelope believe that White Antelope may have confiscated the blanket during a raid into Navajo country.

White Antelope was one of the first to fall when Colonel John Chivington's volunteers descended on the peaceful Cheyenne encampment at Sand Creek in 1864. Hearing gunfire, the chief emerged from his lodge with his hands upraised, palms forward—the traditional sign for peace. As bullets fell around him he folded his arms and began chanting (continued on page 100)

*Navajo weavers from Ramah,
New Mexico, at the IARC, 1988.*

the death song: "Nothing lives long, / Nothing lives long, / Except for the earth and the mountains…" The Sand Creek Massacre stands as one of the most tragic and brutal events in American history. Most of the estimated two hundred killed were women and children, although Colonel Chivington claimed to have killed five to six hundred Cheyennes out of a "hostile" force of nine hundred.

Officer John R. Tritts reported that trooper Henry Mull took the blanket from White Antelope's body on the massacre field and sold it to George Clark, a businessman and future mayor of Denver, for $300. Clark wore the blanket as a raincoat for several years when he was a driver for the Overland Express. His daughter, Mrs. W. G. Wiggington, inherited the blanket from him and sold it to the Indian Arts Fund (IAF) in 1929 for $2,500. Kenneth Chapman and H. P. Mera spent considerable time raising funds to acquire the piece— testimony to their confidence in its authenticity and importance.

In the 1940s the Cheyenne tribe learned of the existence of the blanket and asked the IAF for its return. After an exchange of letters, their request was turned down. In 1996 Cheyenne elders Gordon Yellowman, Sr., and Lightfoot Hawkins contacted the IARC and inquired about the blanket. IARC director Michael Hering invited them to come to Santa Fe

Cheyenne visitors in Washington, D.C., 1851 or 1852. From left, White Antelope, Alights on the Cloud, Little Chief.

to discuss issues related to ownership and access. After their visit, Yellowman requested that the blanket be brought to the Cheyenne and Arapaho Reservation in Oklahoma, where it could be viewed by Chief Joe Antelope, White Antelope's grandson, along with other tribal elders, relatives, and chiefs.

Joe Antelope was ninety years old and in declining health when IARC representatives brought the blanket to Watonga, Oklahoma, in February 1997. The largest assemblage of Cheyenne elders and chiefs in recent memory gathered at the Indian Baptist Church to recite prayers and sing songs as the blanket was passed through the purifying smoke of a braided rope of sweetgrass. Chief Joe Antelope described how his grandfather was "downed by the soldiers" as he stood praying in front of his lodge. He said the blanket was then "stolen away." He added, "Maybe someday the blanket will be put to some good purpose."

Chief Joe Antelope passed away in May 1997. In accordance with his wishes, SAR and the tribe are cooperating to ensure that the odyssey of the Chief White Antelope blanket will continue, both as a tribal icon of the Southern Cheyenne and as an artistic masterpiece preserved for the appreciation of future generations of scholars and the general public.
Duane Anderson

Southern Cheyenne chiefs and elders with the Chief White Antelope blanket, Watonga, Oklahoma, 1997. Seated, from left: Connie Hart Yellowman, Christina Yellowman, Joe Antelope, Alfrich Heap of Birds, Lawrence Hart. Standing, from left: Berniece Armstrong, IARC director Michael Hering, Gordon Yellowman, Bill Eaglenest, SAR vice president Duane Anderson, Lightfoot Hawkins, Larry Roman Nose, Edward Starr, Delbert Hail.

Embroidered Manta

Possibly Tesuque Pueblo
IAF.T44
Length: 106.6cm Width: 149.8cm
Acquired in 1929

Pueblo embroidery is an ancient tradition. Early Spanish explorers reported meeting Native people wearing clothing that was painted and embroidered. Ancient Pueblos also used brocading, a loom technique that resembles embroidery. A few late prehistoric fragments have been found in Arizona, but none used the stitch common today, which is unique to Pueblo work: a pair of yarns is twisted together and the embroiderer inserts the needle between warp threads, passing it back several warps and up between the paired threads. A large area can be covered quickly using this technique.

The design on this piece includes areas of negative pattern—that is, the embroidery yarn provides the background and the design appears in the undecorated ground cloth. This play between positive and negative is characteristic of Pueblo pottery designs as well. The border designs are predominantly traditional Pueblo geometric motifs, with additional flowerlike elements that may have been adapted from Spanish textiles.

The manta, or dress, is a common item of clothing from at least late prehistoric times. Although only a few fragments of textiles survive from ancient sites, kiva murals show us how

people dressed in the fourteenth and fifteenth centuries. The form and decoration of this manta are traditional. The use of wool, however, is a Spanish innovation; all pre-Columbian textiles were woven from apocynum (Indian hemp), yucca, or cotton. The manta is one piece, wider than it is long, and could be wrapped around the body and sewn down one side with the ends over one shoulder or wrapped around the body like a cloak. The top and bottom edges received the majority of the decoration. When worn as a one-piece dress, the plain black area would fall at the center of the body and be bound by a sash or belt. Today the manta is worn only for dances and other ceremonial events. *Marian Rodee*

*Hopi Buffalo dancers at San Juan
Pueblo, ca. 1935.*

Chief Blanket

Navajo, 1860
IAF.T71
Length: 190.5cm Width: 142.2cm
Acquired in 1930

The most famous of all Classic blanket patterns is the "chief" design, so named by non-Navajos because it seemed to be popular with men of rank. Chief blankets exist in three variations or phases. Phase I blankets, the simplest, contain three bands of alternating indigo and red stripes set against a field of broad black and white stripes. Phase II textiles have bars or other simple motifs in the bands, and Phase III features large diamonds that frequently extend into the field. A Phase IV with large oversize diamonds is occasionally found.

In an overly tidy but logical categorization, the example shown here is called a "Phase Two and a Half" because it doesn't quite conform to a Phase II pattern and the diamonds are small and multiple. It can be regarded as a step toward the elaboration of a fully developed Phase III textile. Even the bars are rather tentative and don't take up the entire width of the band, and the "diamonds" are merely opposed triangles. While the system of classification is useful, there is no evidence that the Navajos themselves thought of an orderly progression of styles.

The chief patterns, especially the most common, Phase III, were extremely popular with Plains Indians, in particular the Cheyenne, who are frequently portrayed wearing them in

ledger drawings. Interestingly, it is the women and not the men who are most often shown wearing the blankets. Nearly all the blankets in museums documented as collected from Plains Indians are in the chief pattern.

In contrast to other Navajo blankets and Hispanic textiles, but like Pueblo textiles, the chief pattern is wider than it is long. The vertical edges of this piece are very wavy, indicating that it was worn for years wrapped around its owner, whose fingers pulled at the edges and caused the distortions. *Marian Rodee*

Cheyenne women wearing Navajo blankets.
Watercolor by Lt. James W. Abert,
U.S. Topographical Engineers, ca. 1845.

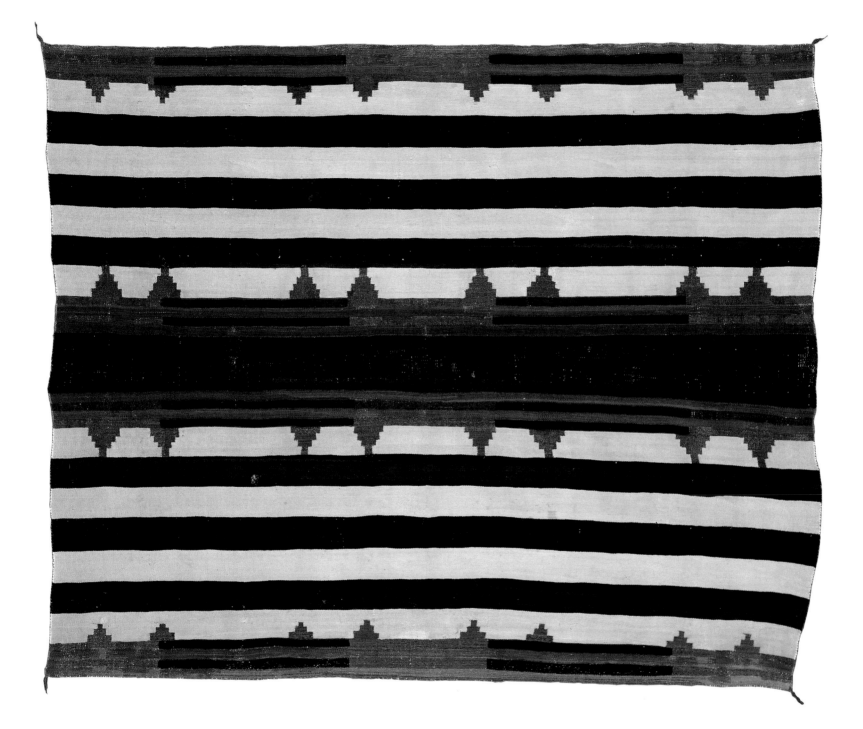

Navajo Sandpainting Rug

Hosteen Klah
Navajo, ca. 1925–30
IAF.T123
Length: 213.4cm Width: 250.5cm
Acquired in 1930

Rugs woven in the designs of Navajo sandpaintings are relatively rare today, and in the 1920s and 1930s they were even more unusual. Older pieces like this one are larger than those being made today. This example is by the famous medicine man Hosteen Klah (Mr. Left Handed), from the Two Grey Hills area of the eastern Navajo Reservation. Klah was weaving when Frances Newcomb, a former schoolteacher with special abilities in painting and drawing, arrived at her husband's trading post at Two Grey Hills. Klah had lost his apprentice and did not want his knowledge to disappear, so he allowed Newcomb to attend his healing ceremonies and draw the elaborate ceremonial paintings executed in sand and plant pollens on the floor of the patient's hogan. Newcomb subsequently suggested that Klah weave sandpainting designs for sale. At first he was concerned that people would walk on the rugs and soil the precious designs given to man by the Holy People. When Newcomb convinced him this would not happen, he began to weave and completed his first textile in 1919. Later Klah made these rugs with his nieces Irene and Gladys Manuelito. This example was woven by Klah and Irene between 1925 and 1930.

Klah was a specialist in the Nightway chant, the inspiration for the radial design of this piece. From the central lake radiate the four sacred plants of the Navajo: corn, beans, squash, and tobacco. In each of the four directions *ye'ii*, or Holy People, stand on rainbows. The central painting is surrounded by a rainbow, and the opening in the east is guarded by Big Fly, who acts as a messenger between this world and that of the supernaturals. Each painting represents a precise moment in the myth associated with the ceremony.

Designs that are more circular and less angular are relatively easy to execute in sandpaintings. Loom technique, with its angular intersection of warp and weft, means that circles are built with many small incremental flat lines or facets. The materials are all handspun. It would take many months to complete a rug of this size and complexity. *Marian Rodee*

Hosteen Klah, ca. 1935.

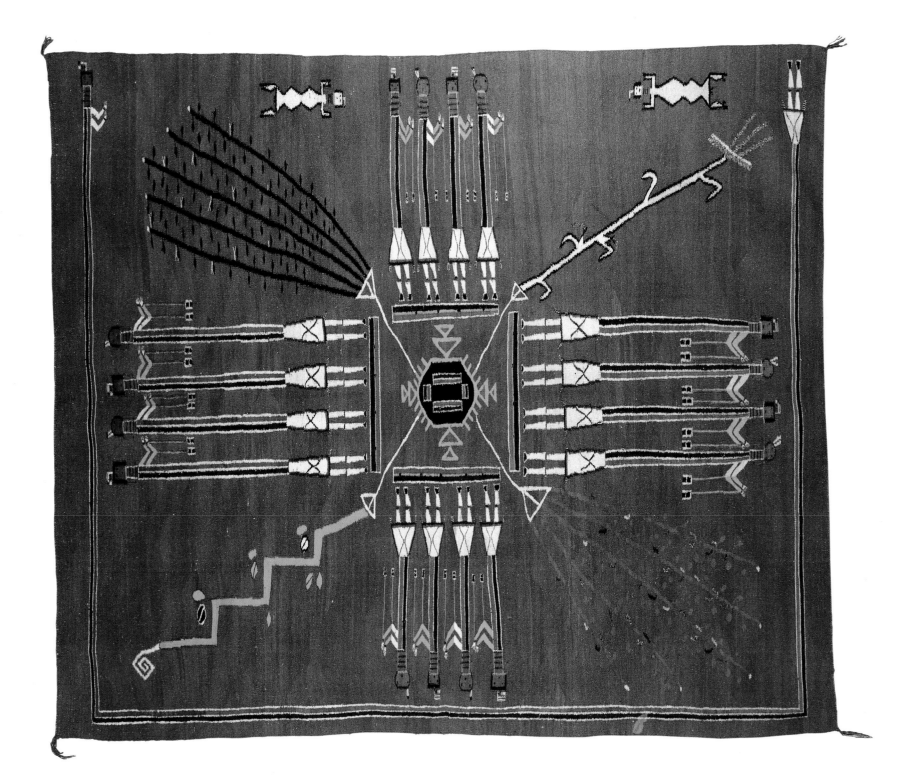

Classic Blanket

Navajo, ca. 1860s
IAF.T175
Length: 205.7cm Width: 147.3cm
Acquired in 1931

This exceptional blanket is known to have been in Santa Fe in the 1860s, when it was in the family of D. H. Browning, U.S. Secretary of the Interior (1865–69). A striking resemblance in the commercial yarns used here to those in the more famous White Antelope blanket have led some to nickname this piece "Son of Chief White Antelope." However, an examination of the weaving technique indicates that the two pieces were not made by the same artist.

The similar elements are the complex pattern and the commercial yarns, with their distinctive subtle color palette. An inaccurate test led to an erroneous report describing both the Chief White Antelope blanket and this piece as Germantown blankets made with synthetic dyes. More recent tests by Casey Reed of Albuquerque have shown that the dyes in these three-ply yarns are totally natural and not anilines. Before the invention in 1857 of the first aniline or coal tar dye, all European dyes were derived from plants, animals, and insect materials. The woolen yarns are of the silky quality known in the nineteenth century as Saxony. The silky appearance of the yarn is probably the result of the processing method used at the

factory, where the wool was pulled through combs dipped in hot wax. The heat burned off the outer scales of the fiber, giving it the smooth appearance of silk in places.

This blanket has been in the shadow of the more historically significant White Antelope piece, but deserves to be appreciated on its own. Its wavy edges are evidence that it was once used as a wearing blanket, suggesting that before being purchased by the Browning family it was probably owned and worn by a Navajo or Plains Indian. *Marian Rodee*

Navajo weavers from Ramah, New Mexico,
at the IARC, 1988.

Handspun Rug

Navajo, ca. 1900–1914
IAF.T400
Length: 203cm Width: 203cm
Acquired in 1943

A new weaving style developed around 1900, believed to be associated with the Hubbell Trading Post at Ganado, Arizona. Trader Lorenzo Hubbell promoted Navajo weaving in his area by commissioning paintings to hang in his rug room, where weavers and customers alike could see the new patterns and designs. Hubbell was fond of Classic blanket patterns and tried to revive them using commercial yarns, but these "Hubbell Revival" rugs did not prove popular with the buying public.

    The large, simple patterns of these textiles, made to be used as floor rugs, are taken from traditional Navajo designs such as the diamonds, bars, and crosses in this piece, floated against a plain background. The backgrounds on most turn-of-the-century rugs are plain white or gray. This one is unusual in being a mottled orange/gray. The carding provides texture as much as hue and enlivens what would otherwise be a large field of plain color. Today, evenness of color is so prized that this spectacular variation of carded wool would not be widely admired. The wool is coarse and "kempy" (with long outer guard hairs), giving it an oriental pile fabric appearance. *Marian Rodee*

*Hubbell Trading Post,
Ganado, Arizona, ca. 1885.*

Rag Rug

Navajo, ca. 1880
IAF.T410
Length: 188cm   Width: 147cm
Acquired in 1944

This rug and nine others were purchased by writer Mary Austin from the daughter of General Chambers McKibben, who was commander of Fort Wingate, Arizona, in the 1880s. All but one of the ten are red, white, and blue, perhaps reflecting the general's military or patriotic inclinations. The pieces can be dated with certainty to the 1880s and were very likely made in the region around the military post.

Only a few of these rag rugs are documented as having been made by Navajos. The rags are actually strips of red baize that were used directly as weft material rather than being pulled apart and re-spun. This reuse of old materials to make floor rugs is a sign of domestic thrift in Hispanic and Anglo households. Rag rug weaving was probably an Anglo introduction, since no such rugs were known among Hispanic weavers before the 1890s. However, Anglo housewives were more likely to braid the strips of old cloth than to weave them. Here, in place of traditional handspun or commercial yarn weft-edge cords, bundles of baize strips are twisted together. The tassels likewise are made of cloth fragments, with bits of green handspun mixed in. The small stripes are of black and white handspun wool, and the warp is brown handspun. Some areas of the cut cloth have a fine blue strip.

Although this piece is relatively coarse for a Navajo rug, it gives the effect of a tufted or pile rug, quite unusual for the Southwest. The pattern is very simple, with three small striped areas and a central diamond. The rug was probably woven quickly, to judge from the simplicity of the design and the coarseness of the materials. The Mexican-flavored design has led some to suggest that this rare piece is non-Indian. *Marian Rodee*

Rug/Blanket

Navajo, ca. 1880s
IAF.T411
Length: 188cm Width: 137cm
Acquired in 1944

Collected by General Chambers McKibben at Fort Wingate in the 1880s, this conventionally woven rug features several small, enigmatic male figures wearing hats with crosses on top. In the late nineteenth century, especially in textiles woven for non-Indians, small human and animal figures often were added to the otherwise geometric patterns. Their meanings, if any, are unclear. To native peoples of the Southwest, the cross is a directional symbol of great antiquity and probably does not denote Christian influence.

The rich, deep red and vibrant green of this rug are striking. Such greens were obtained by mixing imported indigo dye with local plants like the rabbitbrush. This green is unusually vivid, or it may appear so because it is set against such a bright red. Although the indigo and green are native handspun and dyed wool, the red is a commercial four-ply yarn called Germantown. Reds are very difficult to obtain from local plants, and in the 1880s Navajo weavers took imported materials such as trade cloth and manufactured yarns to obtain this much-desired color.

The allover linked diamond pattern is that of a wearing blanket, but the size and weight of the piece indicate it was probably intended to be a rug. When asked to make floor coverings, weavers used the old wearing-blanket motifs and simply increased the size and thickness of their weaving. Notice how the weaver has used only half crosses along the edges, as if the pattern had been cut from a bolt of yard goods. This interrupted or discontinuous pattern is very typical of Classic weaving. In later rugs the use of a border to define and limit the design becomes more prevalent. *Marian Rodee*

Germantown Saddle Blanket

Navajo, ca. 1885–95
IAF.T489
Length: 94cm   Width: 65cm
Acquired in 1952

This is a splendid example of the Germantown or eyedazzler style. "Eyedazzler" is an old traders' and collectors' term, originally derogatory, for the profusion of bright aniline colors and complex patterns that appeared in late-nineteenth-century Navajo weaving.

Weaving of this period still served many of the old functions. This traditional saddle blanket makes use of new materials, including four-ply commercial yarns with synthetic dyes from Germantown, Pennsylvania. The weaver no longer had to shear her wool and spin and dye it but could sit down at the loom with the prepared materials and immediately begin to design and create. This led to a real explosion of color and the so-called outline style, in which each design is outlined with another color.

Since weavers worked without drawings or cartoons, this kind of interlaced pattern would have been very difficult to think through and execute. The weaver has added elaborate tassels and fringe that would hang out the back of the saddle. Small saddle blankets such as

this one could also be thrown over the saddle rather than placed under it. Navajos spent a lot of time and money ornamenting their horses with beautifully woven blankets, silver bridles, and headstalls—jewelry for the horse.

Dealers have recently started to call these pieces "Sunday saddle blankets," although Navajos of the nineteenth century did not necessarily dress in their best to attend church and Sunday school. More likely, they would have used such blankets when going to sings and other important occasions. *Marian Rodee*

Navajo weaver Pearl Sunrise
at an SAR Open House, 1987.

Two Grey Hills Rug

Navajo, ca. 1954
IAF.T646
Length: 238cm   Width: 150cm
Acquired in 1963

Navajo weaving started to gain widespread recognition in the twentieth century. Licensed government traders began settling among the Navajos after the signing of the 1869 peace treaty that set apart their reservation lands. Gradually, trading posts were established all over the reservation at the request of the Navajo people.

One such eastern post was Two Grey Hills, built in 1897 on the site of an ancient Anasazi settlement. Ed Davies at Two Grey Hills and Charles Bloomfield at the neighboring post of Toadlena worked together to develop a distinctive rug with colors and patterns to suit the tastes of Euro-American customers. Oriental rugs were popular in the U.S. at the time, and traders encouraged weavers to incorporate some of their elaborate patterns along with ancient pottery designs found in sherds throughout the region. This style appeared first at Crystal, New Mexico; when it proved popular with buyers, other traders introduced it to their weavers at Two Grey Hills, Teec Nos Pos, and, eventually, Ganado.

Two Grey Hills rugs are known for their simple, natural colors of black, white, and brown, with all the shades in between, and their very complicated patterns. The style developed in the second decade of the twentieth century and has remained virtually unchanged. In this fine example of the Two Grey Hills rug at midcentury, the wool is well spun and the pattern is exuberant and imaginative, with an abundance of filler motifs. The four corners of the rug are emphasized with whirling, starlike patterns. The overall X is used effectively to divide the rug into two bilaterally symmetrical halves. This rug is of exceptionally large size. Technical virtuosity is admired in the Two Grey Hills rugs of today, but this older example demonstrates a more dynamic design than many contemporary pieces.
Marian Rodee

"Trading Post." Painting by Beatien Yazz, 1946.

Teec Nos Pos Rug

Navajo, ca. 1945
SAR.1984-4-64
Length: 353cm   Width: 201cm
Acquired in 1984

A unique style of weaving developed around 1920 in the region around Teec Nos Pos, a trading post in the Four Corners region, where Arizona, Utah, Colorado, and New Mexico meet. Teec Nos Pos means "circle of cottonwoods."

This rug has much in common with the Two Grey Hills piece of the 1950s illustrated in the preceding plate. Both are large and very elaborate floor rugs, and both are based on the new oriental rug patterns introduced by traders. Here, the elaboration of the pattern is emphasized by the multiplicity of colors, something not found in Two Grey Hills textiles with their combinations of black, white, and brown. Teec Nos Pos styles are unique in Navajo weaving and were not emulated by weavers elsewhere. Until recently they were not popular with collectors, perhaps because their strong colors and large, bold, geometric patterns make them less easily adaptable to modern interiors.

Teec Nos Pos rugs often look as if the pattern has exploded, albeit in an orderly manner, over the surface of the rug. The design is divided into thirds, with the top and bottom portions the same. The white lines look like one continuous and fluid ribbon. The small areas of bright colors are commercial yarns, while the other colors are Navajo handspun.

This large floor rug was collected by Margaret Moses, one of the original Fred Harvey girls in the 1920s. Mrs. Moses left her entire collection to the School of American Research in 1984. *Marian Rodee*

Pueblo Embroidered Loincloth

Shawn Tafoya
Santa Clara Pueblo, 1996
SAR.1996-3-10
Length: 178cm   Width: 43cm
Acquired in 1996

Embroidery is still practiced today among the Pueblo people, but it rarely is sold outside the villages because most of the traditional garments that are produced are needed for ceremonies. This striking textile is a man's loincloth with wool embroidery on a commercial cotton fabric known as monk's cloth. Loincloths such as this are sometimes used in dances as banners for kiva groups and are waved over the rows of dancers by a kiva leader. The difference between this textile and a nineteenth-century manta is primarily in the materials used. Very few embroiderers today weave their own ground cloth, and most use commercial yarns in place of the handspun or dyed materials in use a century ago. Designs and techniques, however, have changed very little.

Shawn Tafoya is an award-winning potter and embroidery artist from the Tafoya family of potters at Santa Clara. He began making art when he was five years old and later developed

his talents at the Institute of American Indian Arts in Santa Fe. As the 1996 Ron and Susan Dubin Native American Artist Fellow at SAR, Shawn was able to study the IARC's textile collection and incorporate new ideas into his own work. He has taught pottery making and embroidery at the Poeh Cultural Center at Pojoaque Pueblo. *Marian Rodee*

Shawn Tafoya at the IARC, 1996.

BASKETS

Coiled Jar

Zuni Pueblo, ca. 1880
IAF.B3
Height: 20.3cm Diameter: 23.5cm
Acquired in 1930

Baskets of this type are rare and are often mistakenly identified as Navajo, Apache, or Paiute, even if they were collected at Zuni or other Pueblo villages. This is because at the time they were collected no similar baskets were being made by the Pueblo Indians, so it was assumed that they must have been made elsewhere.

In 1883 and 1888 James and Matilda Cox Stevenson collected many baskets at Zuni Pueblo for the Smithsonian Institution. Nearly all were plaited wicker, undecorated, and utilitarian. Rare, finely coiled specimens such as the one illustrated here were so unusual that they were believed to have been acquired from other tribes. But which tribes was difficult to determine since they are unlike those made by any other group in the region.

These baskets are distinct in their shape, their design, and most of all, the way they were manufactured. The fine coils consist of two slender rods of scraped willow or sumac with a bundle of yucca fiber, bound together with narrow, noninterlocking splints of willow or sumac. The direction of work is from right to left, and the flat rims are finished with fine herringbone plaiting. The distinctive netlike design is created with splints dyed brown-black.

There is some evidence to suggest a Pueblo origin for these unique baskets. Although the two-rod and bundle construction was used in recent times only by the pre-1900 Navajos, the technique is one of the oldest in the Southwest and was employed by the Anasazi from precontact Basketmaker times until at least 1750. Surviving specimens like this one are well worn, particularly on the rims and the bases. The Zunis say that these baskets are "old" and that they were used for ceremonial purposes such as holding sacred medicines and pollen. Specimens collected around the turn of the century may already have been cherished antiques. *Andrew Hunter Whiteford*

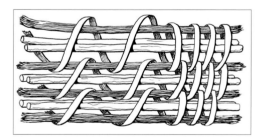

The two-rod and bundle coiling technique.

Burden Basket

Pueblo, ca. 1850
IAF.B15
Height: 30.5cm   Diameter: 30.5cm
Acquired in 1930

This rare basket is significant because so little is known about its type. A dozen of them occur in Santa Fe collections, but they are poorly documented. Kenneth Chapman collected one at Acoma in 1920; several in the Arizona State Museum were obtained by a resident trader at Zuni Pueblo between 1900 and 1923; and two were found in a cache under the floor of an old house at Acoma in 1963. The six specimens at the School of American Research were obtained by members of the Indian Arts Fund from the Western Pueblo villages and represent a distinctive type of burden, or carrying, basket. They appear to be old and used, are often coated with remains of food on the interior, and are unlike anything made by contemporary Pueblo people.

Museums usually classify such baskets as "unknown" or "Apache" because they have the bucket shape and twined weave of Apache burden baskets. Apache baskets, however, are decorated with colored buckskin bands and fringed strips around their rims and down the corners. There are also differences in construction. Apache baskets are made with two rim rods, one of which is frequently of galvanized wire. Pueblo baskets, in contrast, have only a single wood rim rod. The upper ends of the warp elements are bent at right angles and plaited in and out of the two or three adjacent warps, forming a series of loops through which a strip of buckskin or a willow splint is passed and wrapped around the rim rod. The finish resembles the rims of Hopi wicker baskets.

Some Pueblo baskets are decorated with encircling bands or blocky geometric figures. Like the Apache baskets, some are reinforced with stout U-shaped rods that usually cross on the bottom and are woven into the corners. In the design seen here, the wefts are neither painted nor dyed but are given a half twist in order to bring the dark bark of the splint to the surface. *Andrew Hunter Whiteford*

Coiled Bowl

Tohono O'odham, ca. 1900
IAF.B21
Height: 17.8cm   Diameter: 47cm
Acquired in 1930

The Tohono O'odham (Papago) people of Arizona's Sonoran Desert live in rancherías with open ramadas in the summer and move into thatched shelters near springs in the winter. Although they practice *akchin* farming (planting corn and other crops along the lower edges of slopes where there is some runoff), their main sources of food are hunting and gathering. Throughout the year they harvest wild crops such as cactus fruits (saguaro, cholla, prickly pear, and agave), along with a variety of nuts, berries, roots, and greens.

The Tohono O'odham also demonstrate their ingenuity and inventiveness in their basketry. Early baskets were sewn with willow, with coils made of strips of yucca or, more often, beargrass. Since willow was difficult to obtain, a good deal of black "devil's claw" fiber was incorporated into the stitching, giving the baskets a dark appearance. The fine example illustrated here has a design that resembles those used by the neighboring Akimel O'odham (Pima), but with a negative pattern and with line elements two coils wide. Tohono O'odham baskets tend to be heavier and stiffer than those of their neighbors, but are equally well made.

Before 1900 the shortage of willow led some Tohono O'odham to substitute splints of yucca leaves for stitching. Initially this innovation was rejected by collectors and dealers, but the tribe formed a fund to support this work. Continuing to experiment, weavers abandoned the tight, compact stitching with unsplit stitches that had been the traditional mark of fine baskets and began to split the yucca stitches deliberately and even to spread them apart in "wheat stitches." This technique produced a new appearance and allowed the green beargrass in the underlying coils to show clearly. Baskets made in this way required less time to create and could be sold for lower prices. By the 1980s they were by far the most common baskets in "Indian arts" stores throughout the Southwest and beyond. The innovation has kept both Tohono O'odham basketry and basketmakers alive. *Andrew Hunter Whiteford*

Tohono O'odham baskets, illustrating positive (left) and negative (right) designs.

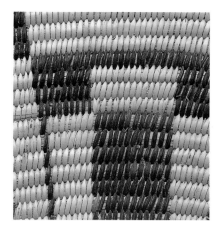

Coiled Bowl

Akimel O'odham, ca. 1900
IAF.B31
Height: 16.5cm Diameter: 45.7cm
Acquired in 1930

The Akimel O'odham people, who live near Phoenix, Arizona, are commonly known as the Pima. Their Indian name, meaning "River People," distinguishes them from their Papago relatives to the south, who are the "Desert People." The O'odham are believed to be the descendants of the highly developed, precontact Hohokam culture that produced large villages, complex irrigation systems, and fine pottery and stonework.

Traditionally the Pima were expert irrigation agriculturists along the Gila and Salt Rivers, until their water rights were preempted by Euro-Americans. Approximately 12,000 Pima still live in the area, where they continue to adapt to change while conserving some aspects of traditional culture. Both O'odham groups were accomplished basketmakers, although the art has almost disappeared among the Akimel O'odham. In spite of the establishment of the Gila River Arts and Crafts Center, few Pima baskets are made for sale, and most of these are miniatures. Fine baskets were still being made around 1950, but in the next decades production narrowed down to little more than souvenirs. By 1980 only a dozen women still knew how to make the old-style baskets.

At its zenith, Pima basketry was a major artistic achievement, as shown by the enormous and impressive collections of Pima baskets found today in museums and private collections. Traditional baskets with characteristic designs are documented as early as 1855 and continued almost without change for a century. As in the piece illustrated here, the most common shape was a large shallow bowl, although a few ollas were also made.

The distinctive Pima technique involved coiling with a foundation of shredded cattail stems wrapped tightly and stitched with narrow splints of willow. The complex geometric designs were sewn with splints of the pods of devil's claw. The stitches were compact—often nearly twenty per inch—and the tight coils ranged from approximately one-eighth to five-eighths of an inch in diameter. The smooth surface thus produced was further improved by beating the basket wall between two stones and rubbing it vigorously with a cloth. The result was a flexible, thin-walled basket with a centripetal design bordered by the black rim and central disk. *Andrew Hunter Whiteford*

Tohono O'odham basketmaker.

Coiled Bowl

Chemehuevi, ca. 1920
IAF.B65
Height: 6.9cm Diameter: 27.3cm
Acquired in 1930

The Chemehuevi are a Numic-speaking people related to the Southern Paiutes of northern Arizona and New Mexico. Most of the surviving Chemehuevis live near Parker, Arizona, at the Colorado River Indian Reservation. During the long periods of migration from their original home near the Nevada border southward along the Colorado River, they retained their language but modified their culture by adopting agriculture from the Mojaves and other Yuman groups. The high development of their coiled basketry technique may have resulted from contact with California tribes, although Chemehuevi designs are unique.

Like those of other Paiute people, Chemehuevi baskets originally were made for utilitarian purposes. When the railroad reached the southern Colorado River valley around 1900, the Chemehuevi began making more technologically and stylistically refined baskets to sell to tourists. The characteristic style was fully developed by the end of the first quarter of the century, and the prices of baskets rose as they became increasingly rare. This specimen illustrates the fine, narrow coiling of three slender willow shoots. They are sewn with fine splints that are split from willow and then sized and smoothed by being pulled through holes punched in the lid of a baking soda can. The typical crisp, discrete, linear designs are executed in black devil's claw splints. The coiling moves from left to right, although this is not true of all Chemehuevi baskets, and the bound rim is characteristically black.

When Chemehuevi basketry was at its height in the 1950s, bowls like this were common, as were small, round-bodied ollas. Many were decorated with naturalistic motifs of butterflies, birds, bugs, and snakes. Each design belonged to the woman who made it. A few colors were introduced, using pink strips from the vanes of red-shafted flicker feathers and yellow and red-brown splints from the roots of the juncus reed. This basketmaking tradition is now nearly extinct. In 1993 only Mary Ann Brown was still producing fine baskets; fortunately, two of her young relatives were learning the art from her. *Andrew Hunter Whiteford*

Coiled Bowl

Havasupai, ca. 1895–1900
IAF.B212
Height: 10.8cm   Diameter: 38.7cm
Acquired in 1941

The Havasupai live in Cataract Canyon at the bottom of the Grand Canyon and are related to the neighboring Hualapai and Yavapai. Traditionally they farmed irrigated plots along Havasu Creek and hunted on the surrounding high plateau. Access to their canyon village is by a steep trail eight miles long, and as a result of this isolation the tribe was largely unaffected by outsiders until the twentieth century.

The ancient Havasupai basketmaking tradition has waxed and waned but is now being revived for the tourist trade. Fine coiled and twined baskets were once used for many purposes—carrying burdens, serving food, and storing water, flour, and other ingredients. In many older baskets the spaces between the stitches still hold remnants of white flour, which has hardened to produce an almost ceramic texture.

This typical early bowl, probably made between 1895 and 1900, was collected by Harry P. Mera, a member of the Indian Arts Fund. Havasupai baskets are tightly coiled, with slender willow splints sewn around a bunch of three narrow rods of three-lobed sumac. The black designs are created with splints from the hard, black pods of the devil's claw. The multipointed central star formed by a ring of outlined diamond shapes is typical, as is the light-colored rim finished with a diagonally plaited herringbone pattern. The rim differs from those of Western

Havasupai basketmaker Minni Marshall, 1974.

Apache bowls, which are wrapped with devil's claw. The pendant triangles inside the rim are also characteristic of Havasupai baskets. The weaver held the basket on her lap with the concave side toward her as she made holes in the coil with her awl and pushed the new splint through to the other face. The "work surfaces" are always very smooth, but the exterior surfaces frequently exhibit uncut fiber threads.

Before the advent of tourists in the Grand Canyon, Havasupai baskets were popular with the Navajos and the Hopis. After tourists began arriving in numbers, the Havasupai made smaller pieces that would sell more readily. A great many of the Havasupai baskets now in collections were obtained in the Hopi villages. They frequently appeared in early photographs of Hopi dances, and for this reason are often identified as Hopi. *Andrew Hunter Whiteford*

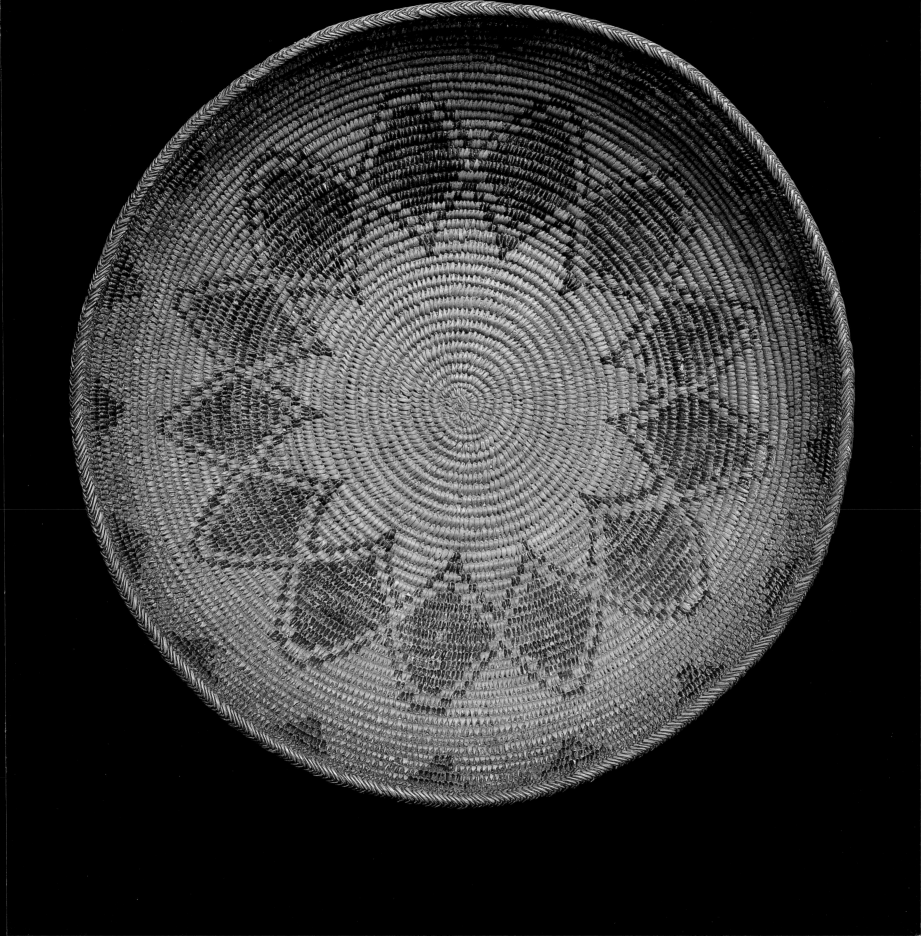

Coiled Bowl
Navajo, ca. 1880
IAF.B252
Height: 11.5cm Diameter: 32.4cm
Acquired in 1941

The Navajos have survived, even prospered, since they migrated to the Southwest prior to 1500. Their rich traditional ritual life is partly responsible for their success. To Navajos, every activity and object is part of the eternal world of the supernatural, a world preserved in legends and songs. Complex rituals are held to restore health and to balance the spiritual forces within both individuals and groups. These ceremonies center around intricate traditional chants that are performed over a number of days.

All traditional Navajo baskets can be regarded as "ceremonial" implements since they are used to hold food, medicines, or colored sands for the sandpaintings created during healing ceremonies. Baskets are also required for lesser rites, such as weddings and house blessings, and are often turned over and beaten as drums. Usually the "singer" who conducts the rite is paid in part with baskets because they are necessary for the cycle of religious ceremonies.

This basket was probably made prior to 1900 and was collected by Harry Mera for the Indian Arts Fund in 1941. It is distinctly Navajo, made with slender coils of two thin willow rods and a bundle of yucca or wood fibers. They are coiled from left to right, with the outside as the working surface, and sewn together with fine splints of three-lobed sumac. The rim is finished with a herringbone stitch that emulates the pattern of the juniper leaves given to a Navajo weaver by the god Haashch'ééíti'i. The top edge of the basket is flat due to the compression of the fiber bundle in the coil.

The design of three crosses, each consisting of four rectangles tipped with small squares, is known as a Spider Woman cross. It was Spider Woman who taught the Navajos to weave, and her crosses often appear on textiles. The diagonal division of the arms of the crosses on this basket is unusual, especially in the use of colors. The Navajos employed a variety of dyes. The black here was probably made with ground coal or roasted ochre boiled with sumac leaves and piñon pitch; the red was produced with juniper roots and bark of the mountain mahogany, with some alder bark and burnt juniper or cedar needles. *Andrew Hunter Whiteford*

Navajo woman holding a basket with black stepped designs. Painting by Beatien Yazz, 1990.

Wicker Plaque

Hopi, ca. 1890
IAF.B282
Diameter: 35.6cm
Acquired in 1949

The Hopis are perhaps the finest and most productive basketmakers in the United States. Their lives on the dry mesas of northeastern Arizona center around the ritual dances, offerings, and prayers that define their relationship with nature and the forces of the complex pantheon of gods and spirits upon whom they depend. A great company of spirits called katsinas are depicted in art and represented by masked dancers in initiation and rain-bringing ceremonies.

The figure on this basket is Crow Mother (Angwusnasomtaka or Tumas), sometimes regarded as the mother of all katsinas, or at least of the whippers who accompany her to maintain decorum when she appears at the great Bean Dances, or Powamu. She goes from

560/650   TEÜ-MAHS
MOTHER OF TWO
HOPI EAST
1926

house to house in each village, accompanied by frightfully masked Nataskas (Monster katsinas) who scare the children and demand food as the price of avoiding punishment for misdemeanors. They are surrounded by Powamu Koyemsi, or Mudheads, who run back and forth carrying the collected food into the kivas.

Baskets serve many purposes in Hopi life. They hold food and ceremonial equipment at rituals, are distributed as gifts at weddings, for newborn babies, and to honor initiates, and are sold to visitors. This basket, which was collected by Harry Mera, is an example of the plaited wicker plaques made only in the villages of Third Mesa. Radiating warps of dunebroom form the base through which strands of dyed rabbitbrush are plaited. Coiled baskets, made only in Second Mesa villages, are very different in construction and materials but are used in the same ways as the wicker baskets.
Andrew Hunter Whiteford

"Crow Mother Kachina." Lithograph by Jo Mora, ca. 1925.

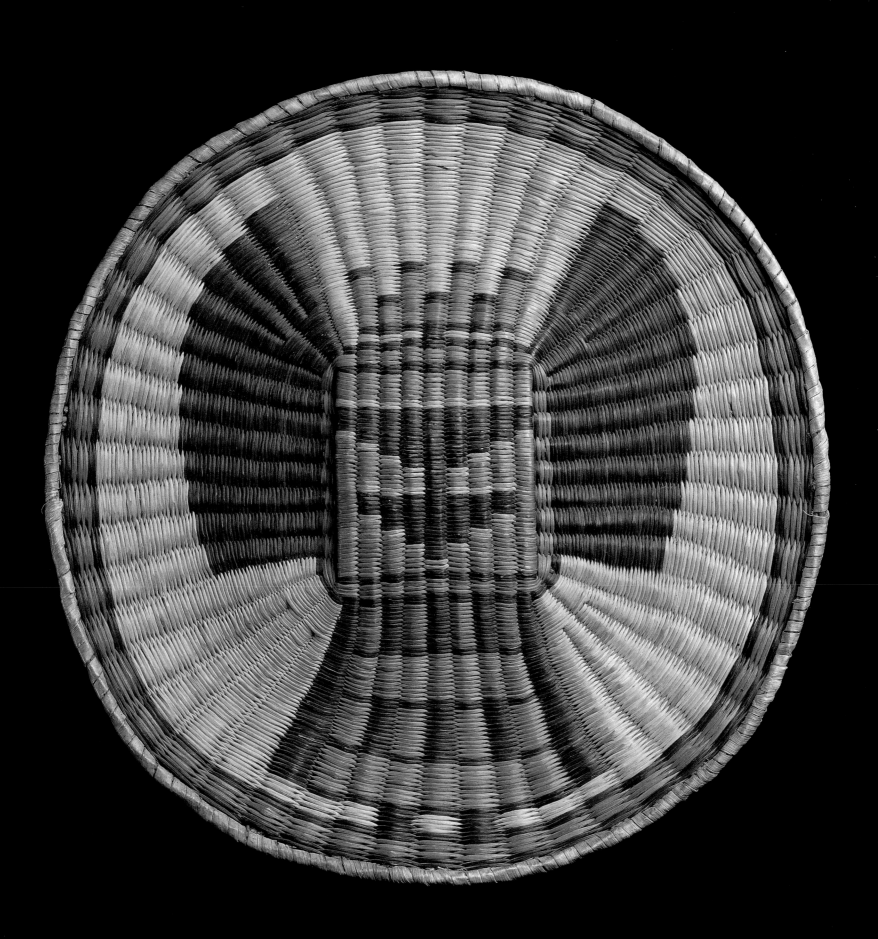

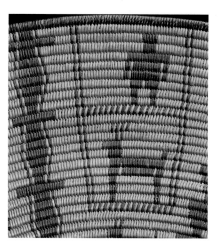

Coiled Bowl
Western Apache, ca. 1890
IAF.B383
Height: 12.7cm   Diameter: 57.8cm
Acquired in 1962

Handsome, shallow bowls like this were once used for winnowing and parching seeds. The early ones were not lavishly decorated. Even before the railroad brought tourists to the area in the 1880s, however, some bowls and ollas were adorned with geometric designs and human and animal figures. By the 1890s the Western Apaches were producing some of the most attractive baskets in the Southwest, and they were eagerly collected by visitors from other parts of the country. Even today, long after production has ceased, they are highly sought after and command very high prices.

The baskets are coiled on a bundle of three slender withes of three-lobed sumac and tightly sewn with fine splints of willow or cottonwood. The contrasting black designs are created with splints from devil's claw seed pods, which are also used on the rim and the start because they are so durable. Typical patterns use curved or straight lines expanding from the center to the rim, frequently consisting of small geometric figures such as the triangles and semidiamond shapes on this specimen. The most interesting motifs are the figures of men, women, horses, deer, and dogs. Usually small, isolated, and surrounded by a frame of narrow lines, they often appear intentionally off-balance. According to the Apaches, these figures have no symbolic or ritual significance.

Western Apache baskets differ in shape, materials, construction, and decoration from those made by Eastern Apaches. Around 1900 Western Apache women made some very large olla-shaped baskets. They sold well, especially to museums and collectors, but their production was time consuming, and smaller baskets were more profitable. Some decorations with touches of red from splints of yucca root appeared about this time and continued to be used, especially in ollas.

Andrew Hunter Whiteford at the IARC, 1982.

For nearly a century (1850–1940) the coiled baskets of the Western Apaches (San Carlos and White River) flourished and provided a constant source of income. During World War II tourism dropped off so much that women virtually stopped making coiled baskets. The production of twined baskets continued for ritual use. Some coiling was reinitiated around 1980, and a slow revival of this once-great tradition is now under way. *Andrew Hunter Whiteford*

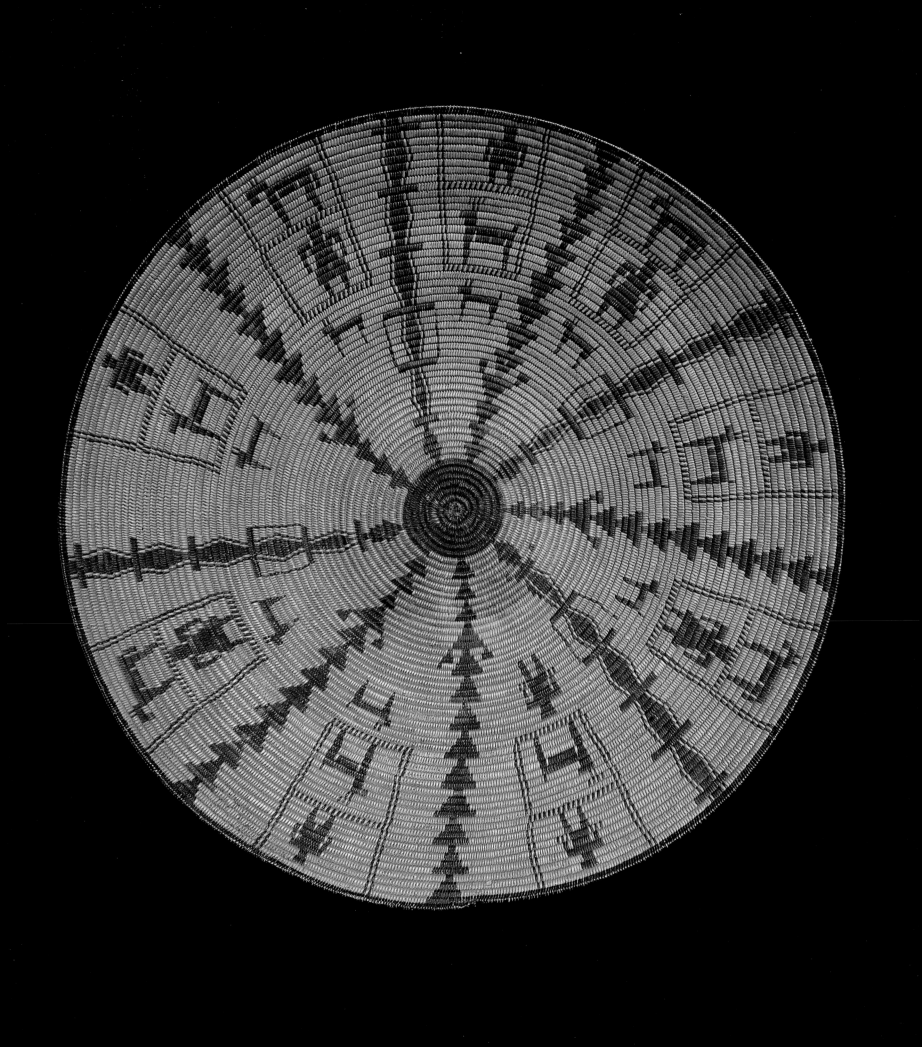

Coiled Bowl with Lid

Tohono O'odham, ca. 1940
SAR.1981-2-18
Height: 9cm Diameter: 33cm
Acquired in 1981

This fine basket, a gift from Sallie Wagner, represents a step in the transformation in Tohono O'odham (Papago) basketry techniques from traditional compact coiling to the new open stitching that produced so many fine yucca baskets. It is a magnificent example of the elegant appearance that can be attained with simple, uncolored, creative stitching. Although the semiglobular shape with a close-fitting lid is unusual, the narrow coils are built of the traditional split cattail stems. The use of willow for the stitching is also traditional but was rarely used after yucca became the prevalent material for sewing baskets. The willow stitches are precisely split with the weaver's awl, producing an ornamental effect. In accordance with the new approach to sewing coiled baskets, the rows of stitches are widely separated from each other and rise from the bottom of the basket to the rim in parallel curved lines that create a subtle design.

Clearly, the weaver who made this basket understood much about the old willow sewn baskets, but she was also able to utilize some new ideas without giving in to the temptation to sew with the more available and easier-to-use yucca leaves. Her creativity and independence are reflected as well in the basket's unusual shape.

Although willow stitching gave way to the exclusive use of yucca around 1900, the old tradition has survived in remote parts of the Tohono O'odham Reservation near the village of Chuichu. Contemporary baskets are meticulously sewn with splints of black devil's claw to create traditional complex squash-blossom patterns as well as nontraditional designs of insects, butterflies, and rattlesnakes. In this same area, and others, baskets are now made with black and white horsehair, beautifully coiled and tightly sewn, often with designs of rattlesnakes and tiny human figures. The baskets are usually small (7 to 10 inches) and almost as hard and smooth as delicate china. They are timeconsuming and demanding to make, but command high prices on the market. *Andrew Hunter Whiteford*

Coiled Bowl

Marilu Lehi
San Juan Paiute, ca. 1984
SAR.1986-7-88
Diameter: 68.5cm
Acquired in 1986

This attractive basket is valuable not only for its beauty but also as a symbol of the remarkable resurrection of a Native American craft. The nomadic Paiutes, who extended from Colorado to California, depended on baskets for their gathering-and-hunting way of life. Their many kinds of baskets for carrying, storing, processing, and serving food were made by coiling or twining, and their beauty depended on shape and texture rather than decoration. Some of the Paiute bands, particularly those around Mono Lake and Lake Tahoe, developed outstanding basketry arts that far outshone the products of their relatives in New Mexico and Arizona.

One small San Juan band of Southern Paiutes lives on the edge of the Navajo Reservation near Hidden Springs, Arizona, where they maintain their own ways and speak their Numic language. They raise corn and wear clothing and jewelry in the Navajo style. They also make coiled "Navajo wedding baskets," which they sell to the Navajos for ceremonies. Life has changed for many in the San Juan band in the thirty years since William Beaver and his Navajo wife, Dollie Begay, owners of Sacred Mountain Trading Post, suggested that weavers start making "old-time" Paiute baskets. Beaver urged them to consult the older women for instruction and brought them books and magazines so they could see what other tribes were doing. Fortunately, 87-year-old Marie Lehi was able to teach the weavers the traditional techniques, and soon they were creating and copying a broad spectrum of designs and producing them in many colors.

The baskets were featured in a major exhibition held in 1985 at the Wheelwright Museum in Santa Fe, where the weavers gave demonstrations, and a generous donor purchased the entire

collection for the School of American Research. Subsequently the Paiutes formed a cooperative to market their newly developed basket arts. Today basketmaking helps the modern Paiutes cope with the surrounding alien culture in a way that parallels the role baskets played in making a living in the harsh desert environment in earlier times. *Andrew Hunter Whiteford*

Fayola Roybal, a Jicarilla Apache basketmaker from Dulce, New Mexico, and IARC volunteer Marianne Kocks examine Marilu Lehi's coiled bowl, 1987.

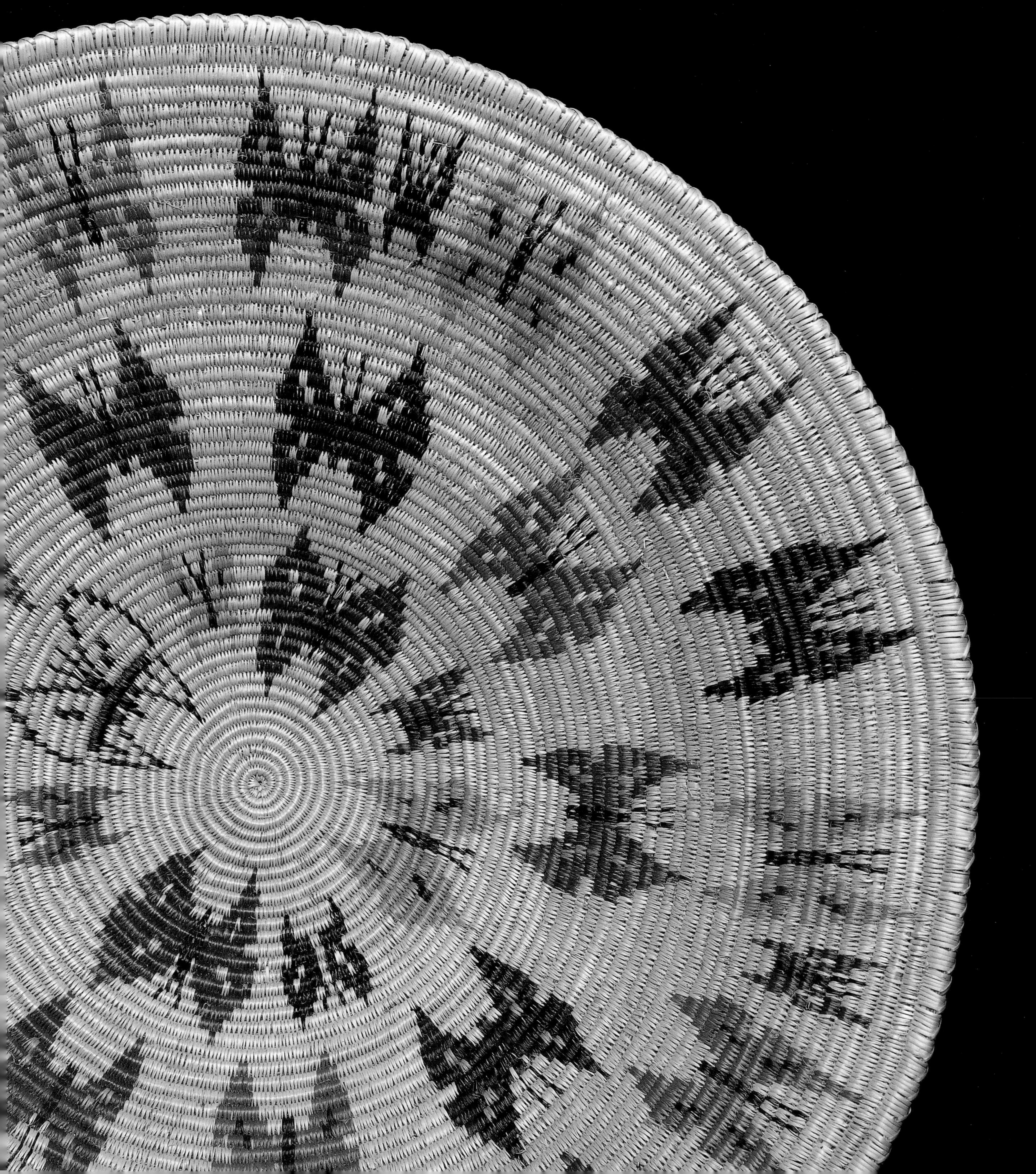

"First Man Placing the Stars"
Coiled Tray
Mary Holiday Black
Navajo, 1997
SAR.1997-8-1
Height: 6.35cm Diameter: 49.53cm
Acquired in 1997

Mary Holiday Black is the matriarch of a venerable dynasty of Navajo basketry artists. Of her eleven children, nine are accomplished basket weavers. Generations of Holiday women have tended sheep, reared children, supervised daily domestic activities, and made coiled baskets for ceremonial use at the family's ancestral home on Douglas Mesa, Utah, adjacent to Monument Valley. Black had begun to experiment with new designs by 1970 and became an important catalyst for innovation in Navajo contemporary basketry. She received the Utah Governor's Award in the Arts in 1993 and the National Heritage Fellowship from the National Endowment for the Arts in 1995. Both honors were in recognition of her major contributions to the perpetuation and revitalization of Navajo basketry arts.

In November 1997 Black was one of ten invited participants in the Southwestern Indian Basketry Artists Convocation at the School of American Research. Each weaver was asked to create a masterwork to enhance the collections of the Indian Arts Research Center. Black's response was "First Man Placing the Stars." In several ways it is a typical Navajo basket. The material for both foundation and coil was collected from the three-lobed sumac bush, and the basket is finished with the conventional herringbone rim. However, the iconography represents a new direction in Navajo basketry design.

The idea for this basket came from Black's father, who was a medicine man. "First Man Placing the Stars" tells the story of the origin of celestial bodies. First Man is carefully placing the constellations in orderly fashion while Coyote, the Trickster, watches. Soon Coyote grows impatient with the meticulous work and randomly scatters the remaining stars. The red star is the "Coyote Star." The day/night, positive/negative aspects of the design reflect the Navajo belief that everything in the universe is composed of complementary and balanced dualities.

Black and her daughters have been making pictorial designs based on portions of the Navajo origin narrative for several years. These "story baskets" can be seen as part of a continuum going back to the beginning of the twentieth century, when ceremonial images first appeared in Navajo textiles. The reinterpretation of ceremonial subjects for use in secular art has since become an acceptable practice. Many women continue to produce coiled baskets for ritual use, thus confirming the vitality of Navajo ceremonialism. The secularized version of the basketry tray provides Black and other Navajo basketmakers with a vehicle for creative growth.
Susan Brown McGreevy

Mary Holiday Black and her daughter, Lorraine Black, at the Basketry Artists Convocation, 1997.

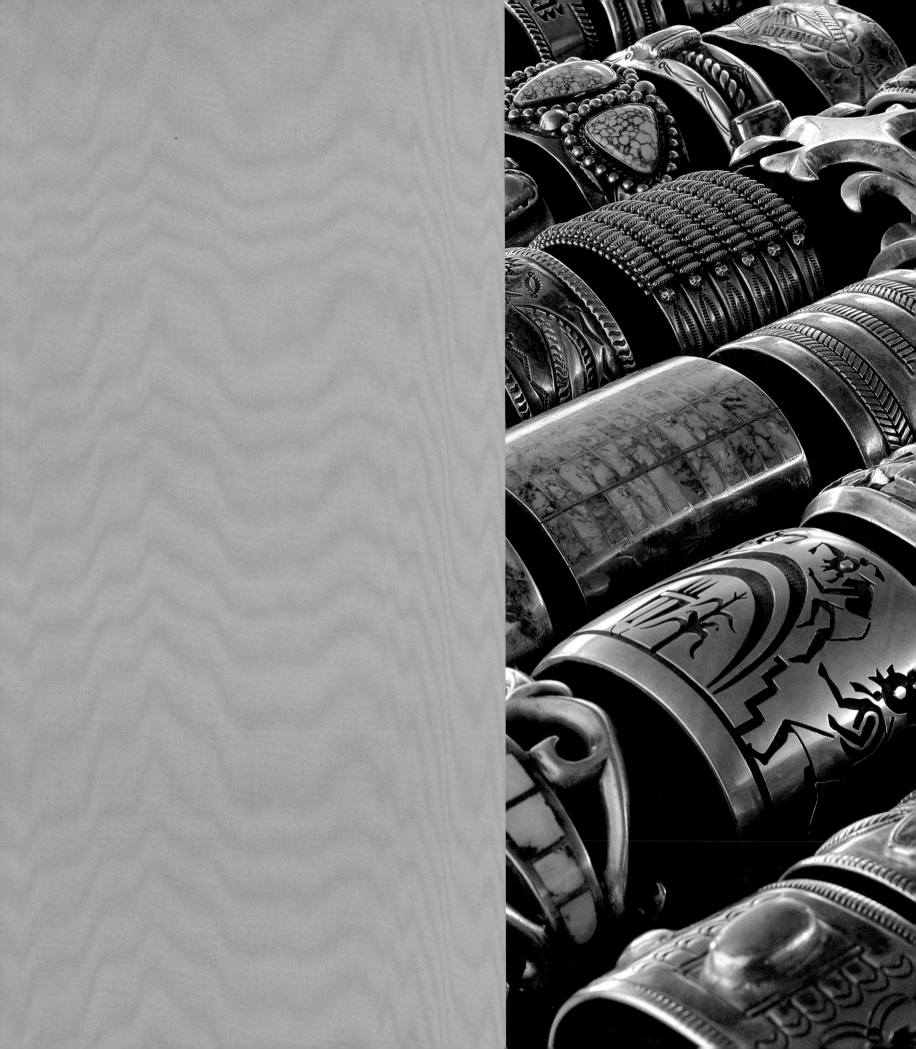

JEWELRY

Bracelet

Navajo, ca. 1887
Coin silver
IAF.S2
Width: 2.3cm
Acquired in 1927

Kenneth Chapman and Harry Mera established the jewelry collection of the Indian Arts Fund when they purchased ten examples of Navajo silverwork in the summer of 1927. The pieces were previously owned by an Indian trader from Durango, Colorado, who probably obtained them directly from their makers in the late 1880s. This bracelet of coin silver (obtained by melting down silver coins) is one of four from that group. Although it appears to be made from a single piece of silver—which may have been the impression the smith was attempting to achieve—it actually comprises three separate lengths of silver. Using what was probably scrap from another project, the smith kept the three sections together by soldering one piece at the inside center and a strip at the outside of each end.

For decoration, silversmiths working around 1880 relied primarily on filing, scribing (cutting with a sharp tool, such as an awl), and rockerwork (rocking a short-bladed chisel from corner to corner while moving it forward along the metal). A few smiths may have been using simple stamps by then, but it was not until finer files and other tools became available through traders that more delicate stamps could be produced.

This bracelet illustrates how a Navajo smith in the late 1880s incorporated two decorative stamps into his work, one in the shape of a crescent, the other a straight edge with finely filed lines. These stamps were used in combination with a punch, a chisel to create a raised square around the dots made by the punch, and a chasing tool that beveled the edges along each of the three lengths of silver. The result is a handsome bracelet with a design that was obviously carefully planned and executed with great precision.

Allison Bird-Romero

Navajo silversmith, ca. 1908.

Necklace

Navajo, ca. 1890
Coin silver and turquoise
IAF.S488
Length: 38.1cm
Acquired in 1941

This coin silver necklace was estimated to be about fifty years old when it was acquired in 1941, partly on the evidence of the partial date "189-" on a coin used to make one of the pendant squash blossoms. Classic in its design, the necklace exhibits traits that account for the great popularity of this style among Navajo and Pueblo people alike. The size of the beads and the large number of squash blossoms (or pomegranates) make it an outstanding example, one that would have been looked upon favorably not only for its beauty but also as a sign of its owner's wealth and status.

The necklace contains forty-seven plain round beads and twenty-four squash blossom beads. The lower portion of each blossom consists of a tube with two lines filed around it. The three extensions coming out from each tube were formed from half-round wire, placed with the flat side on the outside. Each extension was further adorned with a rounded drop of silver soldered to its end.

The main feature of this necklace is a double *naja* (crescent-shaped pendant), cast in two pieces in tufa stone. A vertical stem at the top of the *naja* was drilled so that the string

holding the beads could run through it, and a twenty-fifth squash blossom was attached upside down above the stem. At the center of the *naja* is a setting of turquoise held by a scalloped bezel. Not quite rectangular in shape, the stone widens slightly at the bottom. Judging from its color, it appears to be Cerrillos turquoise from New Mexico, and may have been a later addition to the necklace. *Allison Bird-Romero*

Navajo woman wearing a silver naja necklace, ca. 1915.

Concha Belt

Navajo, ca. 1875
Coin silver and turquoise
IAF.S561
Length: 105cm
Acquired in 1945

Concha (often referred to as "concho") tests the ability to be creative working within a prescribed form. The silversmith must be able to replicate the concha several times.

Many older belts are described as "classic" in their shape and design. This belt fits in this category, but exhibits variations that set it apart. It features a well-designed buckle and eight oval conchas, each hammered from a coin silver ingot. The buckle is a rectangle with curving, upturned corners and a leaf-shaped form, a common design in Navajo belts of the period. Here, however, the silversmith chose not to repoussé (raise) the corner elements. Instead, two flat, diamond-shaped green turquoise stones are the focus of attention. Stampwork in the unusual shape of four-pointed stars was placed around the buckle's rectangular center opening.

The individual conchas were manufactured in a series of labor-intensive steps. After heating each ingot and hammering it flat, the silversmith cut the scalloped edge and raised the center portion into an oblong-oval shape using the technique of repoussé, which was also applied to each section radiating out from the central oblong-oval. The braided oval surrounding that portion of the design was made by raising the silver with a chisel, then stamping each curved line. The holes on the conchas were made with a punch, and the three lines between the holes were produced by the two stamps of different lengths. *Allison Bird-Romero*

A group of Navajos, ca. 1890.

Ketoh (Bow Guard)

Navajo, ca. 1880
Silver and turquoise
IAF.S696
Length: 8.6cm Width: 6.6cm
Acquired in 1948

The bow guard was originally a plain strip of hide, about four inches in width, that was wrapped around the wrist to protect it from the bowstring. Navajo smiths quite likely began to ornament their bow guards, which they called *ketohs*, sometime in the 1860s. The *ketoh* was a purely utilitarian object that retained its original purpose long after silversmiths began elaborating it. Today, ornamented bow guards remain an important piece of decorative jewelry worn on special occasions by Pueblo as well as Navajo men.

The silver ornamentation on this *ketoh* was cast in tufa stone by a silversmith who was technically proficient, as evidenced by his ability to pour such a thin casting with a relatively complex design. Although it was cast, it has a quality that might be considered delicate when compared with the majority of old *ketohs* produced by the same method.

The design of this piece is reminiscent of the stylized plant forms so often found in early Navajo silverwork. It contains elements more commonly seen in *ketohs* that were made from a single piece of silver using the repoussé technique. In order to highlight certain portions of the design, the smith stamped a series of lines around the outside edge that frames the silverwork. He also stamped these lines along the curved elements radiating out from the oval turquoise stone in the center. The stone, which is quite likely Morenci turquoise, is held by a hand-filed bezel. It is possible that the stone was originally blue and changed to green with time.

The silverwork on this piece exhibits evidence of much wear, as does the ornamented leather wristband to which it is attached. Close examination reveals that the leather was randomly stamped with small, flowerlike forms and larger forms that may have been intended to represent leaves.
Allison Bird-Romero

Bow guards from the SAR jewelry collection.

Dress Ornaments
Zuni Pueblo, ca. 1950
Ingot silver and turquoise
IAF.S755
Height: 11.5cm Width: 8.9cm
Acquired in 1954

These large, matching ornaments are an outstanding example of jewelry created by Zunis for Zunis in the 1950s. Such ornaments, worn by traditionally dressed women for dances or special events such as the Gallup Inter-Tribal Indian Ceremonial, are still highly desired; if a woman does not own jewelry, she borrows it from other family members for special occasions.

These particular ornaments are referred to as "tie-ons" because they lack pin backings and were attached to the manta (dress) only temporarily. They consist of Stinich turquoise mounted on an elegantly simple base of rolled ingot silver. The backing is open, exposing the unpolished reverse side of the stones. The silversmith probably created the lacy scalloped edge by using a hand-cranked drill and then soldering a circle of round wire over each hole.

Lone Mountain turquoise from Nevada was once the favored stone of Zuni jewelers, but by 1950 it was being replaced by Stinich turquoise, also from Nevada. Stinich became popular because it was the shade of blue that the Zunis preferred and because the size of the nuggets being mined at this date allowed for the production of large slabs. The settings on these ornaments are exceptionally large by the standards of the 1950s. The silversmith who created these dress ornaments was well aware of the beauty of the stones and knew that the simplest of settings was all that was needed to frame them. He stamped his heart-shaped hallmark on the back of each piece; unfortunately, his identity is unknown. *Allison Bird-Romero*

Necklace

Tesuque Pueblo, ca. 1880
Coin silver, brass, and beads
IAF.S853
Length: 33cm
Acquired in 1964

Cross necklaces have been a favorite form of ornament among Pueblo and Navajo people for generations and are often family heirlooms. This example was purchased in 1964 by members of the Indian Arts Fund from its owner, Lorencita Pino of Tesuque Pueblo. She reported that it had been in her family for four generations.

Cross-shaped images of dragonflies are commonly found on pottery and in the rock art of precontact Puebloan groups of the Southwest. In the mid-1500s, when the Spanish arrived in the region bearing double-barred crosses made of silver and other metals, that form of cross was readily accepted. The Spaniards hoped that the Indians would adopt the crosses as symbols of Christianity, but most saw them simply as a variation of the familiar dragonfly motif.

Strung on cotton string, this necklace features a large, coin silver, double-barred cross as the main pendant, along with ten smaller coin silver crosses, brass beads, and glass "white heart" trade beads. White heart beads came in varying soft shades of red and orange, with a white inner core. They were popular among the Pueblos because they resembled highly desired coral beads, which were costly and not always available.

The large cross was made from a single piece of silver decorated with simple stampwork. There is a small flower on a stem on the stylized heart at the bottom, and above it a tubular white heart bead placed in the style seen on rosaries. The small crosses were probably made of scrap silver, since their arms were soldered on. Each cross has a twisted top with a hole punched through it for hanging. In form and decoration, the large cross is comparable to a style that was being worn in the northern Rio Grande Tewa pueblos by 1880. The crosses for this necklace may have been manufactured in this area, as similar crosses have been noted on photographs of Tewa people from several villages after 1880. *Allison Bird-Romero*

Tom Toslino (Navajo), 1882.

Box

Zuni/Navajo, ca. 1925
Silver, turquoise, jet, spiny oyster, and mother-of-pearl
SAR.1984-4-72
Height: 4.5cm Length: 13cm
Acquired in 1984

The lid of this outstanding silver box features a well-executed mosaic dragonfly motif made of turquoise, jet, spiny oyster, and mother of pearl. Boxes of this kind were rare, and not every silversmith was capable of making them. Although sometimes overlooked, such decorative objects are an important aspect of Indian metalwork, offering many opportunities for embellishment.

With the encouragement of traders, Navajo smiths began to manufacture decorative boxes and other nonwearable objects of silver for the tourist trade around 1900. Initially the boxes were rather small, but larger examples were produced later with the availability of sheet silver and improved methods of rolling out ingot silver. The larger boxes provided opportunities for the creation of more elaborate stamped patterns and stone settings that would be too large to incorporate into jewelry.

In the 1920s Zuni traders saw the potential for combining Zuni lapidary work with Navajo silverwork. Most Zunis preferred cutting stones and shells for mosaic or channelwork, so by combining the Zuni forms with Navajo-made silver, popular new varieties of jewelry and decorative objects were produced. The trader usually obtained the mosaicwork first and then ordered an item from a Navajo smith that was designed to accommodate it. This box is an example of such a collaboration. It rests on four silver button "feet," and the underside features an arrowhead-shaped hallmark or "signature." *Allison Bird-Romero*

Rainbow Man Pin

Zuni Pueblo, ca. 1930
Silver, jet, turquoise, spiny oyster, and mother-of-pearl
SAR.1988-6-81
Height: 12cm Width: 10.2cm
Acquired in 1988

The world outside the Pueblo of Zuni first learned of Rainbow Man when he was discussed and illustrated in the U.S. Bureau of Ethnology's annual report for 1880–81. It was probably not until the latter part of the 1920s or the early 1930s, however, that Rainbow Man and similar figures important in Zuni ceremonial life were first used as decorative features in jewelry, probably at the suggestion of a Zuni trader. Depictions of all ceremonial figures soon were in demand among tourists and other purchasers of Native jewelry, and Rainbow Man was one of the most popular.

Over time, the work of individual artists became recognizable by the choice of materials, the various ways these were placed within the figures, and, for Rainbow Man, the way the

figure curved to present a stylized depiction of the rainbow. Jewelry featuring Rainbow Man continues to be popular today. Some of the Rainbow Man design characteristics developed by the earlier lapidaries are carried on in the work of their descendants. Other contemporary jewelers have created completely new versions of this figure.

In this pin, jet, turquoise, spiny oyster, and mother-of-pearl were used to adorn Rainbow Man's ceremonial kilt, moccasins, and terraced hat with prayer feathers. Clearly, the artist who created this graceful and detailed mosaic pin was an experienced and talented worker of stone and shell.
Allison Bird-Romero

Zuni Rainbow Man bolo ties
from the SAR collection.

Shalako Altar Set

Zuni Pueblo, ca. 1940
Silver, turquoise, coral, jet, abalone, and mother-of-pearl
SAR.1989-7-166
Height: 7.5cm Width: 7.9cm
Acquired in 1989

This small Zuni Shalako katsina altar set combines exceptional silver and lapidary work. Both jewelry and sculpture, it is truly a piece of wearable art, for what appears to be a single item is actually four pieces of jewelry: the back section of the altar is a bolo tie, the Shalako figure is a pin, and the two front sections are earrings. The patterns are made of turquoise, coral, jet, mother-of-pearl, and abalone shell set in silver channelwork.

The Shalako figure resting at the foot of the altar is patterned after the brightly painted wooden structures that are prepared for important Zuni religious celebrations. Ten-foot-tall Shalako katsinas are the principal gods represented at the winter house-blessing ceremony, a six-week reenactment of Zuni emergence and migration beliefs that begins the first week in December. This highly complex event—a communal prayer for rain, the health and well-being of the people, and the propagation of plants and animals—culminates in the arrival of the Shalakos in the village. Lasting throughout the night and into the next afternoon, the ceremony includes prayer, dancing, and visitations by numerous other katsinas.

Participants at the Pueblo Mosaic Jewelry Artists Convocation held at the School of American Research in February 1997 admired this altar set for its fine craftsmanship, its materials, and the lively expression of the Shalako katsina. According to Zuni jeweler Alex Boone, the piece was probably made before 1940 and may have been created at the suggestion of C. G. Wallace, the main trader at Zuni at the time. "It certainly would have tested the skill of the artist," Boone said. Andrew Dewa, another Zuni jeweler, noted that, due to its subject matter, this altar set was undoubtedly a specially commissioned piece.
Allison Bird-Romero

KATSINAS

Wukomochovi Katsina
Hopi, ca. 1900–1920
IAF.C253
Height: 32.4cm
Acquired in 1952

This katsina is variously known as Wukomochovi (Big-Mouthed katsina), Wuyaq Ho (Big-Headed katsina), and Hölö-okong (Bull Snake katsina), from the snake painted around the eyes of the mask. Wukomochovi is a disciplinarian who comes during the Qöqötinumya or Powamu parade on Third Mesa. As the procession passes each kiva, more katsinas emerge; many of these are the Ichivota, or Angry katsinas, such as Sotuknangu, Chaveyo, and Wukomochovi. Their job is to guard the moving line of Chief katsinas and prevent onlookers from interfering with the march. The entire group makes four circuits of the village; during the last circuit they change direction, going counterclockwise, and the katsinas disappear back into their kivas.

Formerly Wukomochovi also appeared when springs were being cleaned of accumulated mud and debris. His role was to ensure that all the men turned out and did their share of work, so he is often portrayed carrying a yucca-leaf switch in his right hand. Dolls of this katsina are extremely rare because he no longer appears. His disappearance may be linked to the split at Oraibi in 1906, when half the population left to found the village of Hotevilla, or, perhaps, to the diminished use of springs. The most likely reason, however, is the death or disappearance of the Snake clan members who impersonated this katsina. He must now be considered one of the Hisot katsinum—"old ones who no longer appear."

The enormous fan of eagle feathers and the breadth of the beard produce a mask that must have been exceedingly heavy. The katsina has the pink forearms and calves always associated with fierce katsinas. The abbreviated costume consists of a wildcat-skin ruff and breechcloth, a blue leather belt with red horsehair hanging from it, and moccasins with fringed anklets. This doll was a gift from Norma Swearingen in memory of Mary Austin.
Barton Wright

Hututu Katsina

Zuni Pueblo, ca. 1900
IAF.C294
Height: 39.4cm
Acquired in 1961

Nearly every important Zuni katsina has an alternate. Often referred to as "older brother/ younger brother," the alternate is essentially a fail-safe device. Thus, when the katsina known as Saiyatasha makes his ceremonial round through the Pueblo of Zuni, stopping to plant prayer feathers at six places, he is accompanied by his "deputy," Hututu.

Led by Shulawitsi, the group includes Saiyatasha and his helper Yamuhakto. Hututu and his Yamuhakto are next, tramping with heavy steps, followed by a number of Salimopiya katsinas with their whistling calls, who race about as guards. Hututu is named for the deep-voiced call of "Hu-tu-tu!" he makes as he strides along. Although not as striking in appearance as his leader, he is still a majestic personage. His actions and purpose seem to be a reinforcement of those of Saiyatasha. This group brings all manner of benefits to the Zuni, including control of weather, protection from enemies, freedom from witches, and long life.

Hututu's eyes extend to his ears, and his small, square mouth is almost hidden behind his ruff. Traditionally, he carries several scapulae in his right hand, and in his left hand a bow. On his back is an elaborate skin quiver. His costume is extensive, with kilt, sash, ordinary shirt, hunting shirt (sometimes now replaced by an embroidered robe), and buckskin cape. His leather leggings are fringed down the front, and his moccasins are decorated. He wears two large painted or inlaid glycymeris shells around his neck and multicolored feathers on the back of his head.

A gift of Elizabeth White, this is a superb example of a Zuni doll from around 1900, when these katsinas were dressed in realistic clothing. The costume was handmade from head to foot, including the tiny leather moccasins. *Barton Wright*

Shalako Mana Katsina

Hopi, ca. 1890—1910
IAF.C321
Height: 27.9cm
Acquired in 1964

Coming in a multitude of roles, the Shalako Mana is without doubt one of the older Hopi *tihu* (katsina dolls). It was the first doll to be collected from the Hopis in 1857 by Dr. Samuel W. Palmer of the U.S. Army, who donated it to the Smithsonian Institution. Shalako Mana dolls were invariably portrayed nude until the late 1890s, when Victorian attitudes overrode Hopi sensibilities and katsina makers began to clothe the dolls.

The Shalako Mana is a female fertility figure whose power over rainfall affects the corn crop and, therefore, the size of the Hopi population. In the traditional Hopi world, each element—rain, corn, and people—is of utmost importance, and each is addressed in ritual and ceremony.

The Shalako Mana may come as the partner of the Shalako Taka, both towering figures nine feet high, wearing enormous tabletas and clothed in eagle feathers from shoulder to ankle. They were called upon when the clouds did not appear and drought parched the land, and their costumes and postures symbolize prayers for rain. The Mana may appear kneeling behind a grinding stone, reducing kernels of corn to a fine flour used in rituals and for food. When she comes during the initiation of new members into the women's Mamzrau Society, she is a mythic reenactment of the creation of corn in its six major types. The Mana may also appear as a puppet grinding corn before an altar, while her sister, the Palhik' Mana, works on the other side.

This Shalako Mana is an excellent example of an early naked doll representing the female body, symbol of reproduction. The tableta represents clouds from all directions, like a prayer repeated over and over. The red arc across the mouth represents the morning sun shining through the rain that is falling in all the colors of the directions. The eyes and body are painted in the blue and yellow of spring and summer. The vertical red stripes on the body may represent the blood of childbirth.
Barton Wright

Woman holding a Mana doll.
Painting by Awa Tsireh, ca. 1930.

Muyingwa Katsina
Hopi, ca. 1900—1920
IAF.C324
Height: 30.5cm
Acquired in 1964

Muyingwa is the Chief of the Nadir, where he sits on Sichomo, the Flower Mound, in the Fourth World below. He wears a mask of the clouds of all six colors, in front of which flutter sacred birds and butterflies. He is the spirit of germination and controls the growth of every domestic plant, especially corn, while Sotuknangu, Chief of the Zenith, controls the growth of wild plants. It was Muyingwa who taught the Hopi about seeds and vegetation and about the use of stone for architecture. As a deity he is never impersonated, although a katsina representing him may appear in the Powamu as a Tusauv, or helper katsina, and in the Mixed Dance.

During the Katsina Cult initiation, Muyingwa, represented by the Powamu priest, enters the kiva in a slow and stately manner. In a low monotone, he recites the tribe's sacred lore about the katsinas, describes their homes in the San Francisco Peaks and in other shrines and springs, and then leaves. The moment he leaves, the three initiating katsinas arrive at the kiva to begin their actions. Each Hopi mesa seems to have a slightly different interpretation of Muyingwa. On Second and Third Mesas he incorporates many attributes of Alosaka, a two-horned germination spirit who is emphasized on First Mesa almost to the exclusion of Muyingwa.

A rare example of a priest rather than a katsina representing a deity, this doll is the Powamu chief in the guise of Muyingwa. He is unmasked and dressed in ordinary clothes, but usually wears a white maiden shawl about his shoulders and a wicker helmet with two long, blue gourd-horns rising from the crown. Each horn is painted with a triple cloud symbol. In the actual performance the back sides of the horns are covered with cotton. The wavy black lines on the face have been variously identified as feathers or reeds. This doll, a gift of Elinor D. Gregg, carries a wooden wedding plaque instead of the more typical long crook, chief's stick, and small water jug. *Barton Wright*

Qöqöle Katsina

Hopi, ca. 1880–1900
SAR.1980-1-8
Height: 16.5cm
Acquired in 1933

Qöqöle has been painted on pottery at First Mesa for at least a couple of centuries. Sometimes called the Pothole katsinas, the Qöqöles appear after the Soyal katsina during the Soyalungu or Winter Solstice ceremony on Third Mesa, which celebrates the return of the katsinas after their six-month absence. On Third Mesa he comes as a group of dancers accompanied by a Qöqöle Mana. With the exception of the Mana, these katsinas may appear with black, blue, red, or yellow faces and are dressed in cast-off Anglo clothing. On Second Mesa Qöqöle may come during initiation years as a line of Qöqölum burdened with baskets of beans or corn sprouts; in other years he appears in the kiva as a pair—one a braggart, the other quiet and shy—who tell a long story about their adventures on the way to Hopi.

The braggart tells how he will bring the Hopi an enormous deer, but the herd stampedes over him and he is left with a tiny fawn. His brother, however, kills an immense deer. As they travel toward Hopi they encounter a flooded wash. The braggart says he will jump over it but is afraid and hesitates. The quiet one runs and easily jumps the wash, but when the braggart tries he falls into the water and his brother rescues him. He is so full of water that when the quiet one jumps on his stomach water squirts so high it drowns birds, which are then stuck on his head. The adventures continue in the same vein until the two reach Hopi.

Very young Hopi children, both male and female, are given small dolls. Most of these are *puchtihu*, flat pieces of wood painted with a head and a suggestion of arms. On rare occasions a half-round or cylindrical doll like this one is found; most of these are from the nineteenth century. This specimen was acquired by Jesse Nusbaum in the 1930s from the Field Museum of Natural History. *Barton Wright*

Paiyatamhoya Katsina
Hopi, ca. 1890
SAR.1980-1-25
Height: 15.2cm
Acquired in 1933

This small, squatting figure is one of many clowns among the Hopi. Individually they are called Tsuku; a group of them is called Chuchkut. The horned, black-and-white striped clowns are the Koshari of the Tewa. Other clowns are all yellow or all white and wear their hair pulled up in three small knots at the top and sides of their heads. The yellow clowns are known as Sikyachuchkut, and this doll is one of them. However, this clown has his own name: Paiyatamhoya. Found only in the Second Mesa village of Mishongnovi, he is easily recognized, for he is the only one whose eyes and mouth show above the red bands across his face.

Paiyatamo is the patron of all clowns, regardless of color or place of origin. He is known as The Youth and is the deity of spring, flowers, music, fun, and male virility; in essence he represents eternal youth and regeneration. This clown, Paiyatamhoya (Little Youth), takes his name from that personage. At Hopi he is also the son of the Sun and in addition goes by the name of Taiowa.

Hopi clowns amuse their audiences, but they are also the keepers of tradition, and their actions are exaggerations of behaviors that are not acceptable in the village. Their role is tightly controlled by tradition, which dictates where they enter the village, how they announce themselves, their behavior toward the katsinas, and their punishment for misbehavior. But within that role the clowns may lampoon anything or anyone, from tourists to village chiefs, from neighboring tribes to quarreling villagers. All actions may be held up for ridicule by the clowns.

Paiyatamhoya's costume is the bare minimum of a black breechcloth and a black-striped yellow body. He wears rabbitskin earrings and usually has a string of oranges or onions for a necklace. The carving of this small figure is characteristic of dolls made around 1900. It was collected in the 1890s by either Reverend H. R. Voth or the trader Herman Volz and sent to the Field Museum of Natural History. The museum later sold many of these dolls to other organizations. *Barton Wright*

Owaqa Katsina

Marshall Lomakema
Hopi, ca. 1960—70
SAR.1989-7-5
Height: 26.7cm
Acquired in 1989

The Owaqa (Coal) katsinas are those who make the black rock (coal) and stir the fires in the mountains. Usually they are harmless, but when their anger is aroused, as it was many years ago, they pull down the high places and burn everything. Today they come in peace, bringing only a small gourd of water for the Chief katsinas to use in dances.

Pauwatiwa, the War Chief of Walpi, ruminating in 1883 about the Coal katsinas, said that it had been many years since their dance had been given. When his grandfather was a boy these katsinas sent word that they were coming, but on the appointed day they did not appear, and shortly thereafter smallpox broke out and killed many villagers. This so angered the people that they took the chief who had announced the dance out into the valley and killed him. Pauwatiwa also stated that the dance was being given "on the occasion of a white man becoming the first and highest ranking chief we ever had. He has chieftaincy in the Chief clan and among the warriors, a thing prophesied to us but something we never expected to see."

Edmund Nequatewa, informant for Harold S. Colton, stated that the Coal katsina came originally from Shungopovi, where it belonged to the Ash Pile Kiva. This kiva was so poor that it could have only one katsina, Owaqa, who came dressed in a worn-out woman's dress and rags. Owaqa was given so often that it became monotonous and no longer appeared. Owaqa is a Chief katsina and, despite Colton's statement that its last appearance was at Mishongnovi in 1899, it still comes on occasion, for example, during the Pachavu in Hotevilla in the 1960s and again at Mishongnovi's Pachavu in 1978.

Owaqa is seldom represented as a doll, but when made there are several variations. This specimen, made in the 1960s by Marshall Lomakema of Shungopovi, was a gift from Henry S. Galbraith. The katsina wears two hawk or raven feathers on his black face. His ruff, formerly made from withered fruit pods of yucca, is made of cornshucks. Around the middle of his black body he wears a girdle of plaited yucca leaves, which the women potters eagerly grab for, as they make the fires very hot and produce well-baked vessels. *Barton Wright*

He-é-é Katsina

Tino Youvella
Hopi, ca. 1950–70
SAR.1989-7-6
Height: 45.7cm
Acquired in 1989

Sometimes called He Wuhti, this katsina is found in precontact sites, in more than one contemporary Pueblo village, and on all three Hopi mesas. Each varies slightly from a core concept, that of a man/woman. She is considered a mighty warrior and leads a long line of warriors into the villages during the Pachavu ceremony.

Among the Hopi there are two versions of the story. One is that a young woman was having her hair put up one morning when she saw enemies approaching. Because the men were out in the fields, she grabbed a bow and arrows and fought off the invaders until the men returned. The other story is that a young man and his new bride were out in his field and were playing by dressing in each other's clothes. The man was having his hair put up in whorls when he saw an enemy approaching. He picked up his bow and arrows and rushed to defend the village until the other men could come from the fields and help. His new bride hid under the pumpkin plants in the field.

Among the Tewa there is a similar figure who differs only in the fact that she has crescent eyes. She is the eighteenth-century warrior woman who led the band of Southern Tewa as they fled from the Spanish. The Zuni have an equivalent form, known as Kothlamana.

He-é-é is always dressed in a black cape with white cornhusk stars, a black woman's dress, and a rain belt. Her hair hangs loose on one side and is wrapped about a wooden hair frame on the other. She has a small mouth and a narrow beard and wears two warrior prayer feathers on her head. She carries a bow in her left hand and a black rattle spotted with white in her right hand. At Third Mesa a narrow fan of feathers is placed vertically on the back of the head; at First Mesa, the fan lies sideways.

This figure, a gift from Henry Galbraith, is characteristic of dolls made in the late 1950s or early 1960s. At the time katsina carvers had just started to show action in their dolls with gesturing arms or bent legs, and the use of real clothing was not uncommon. *Barton Wright*

Hopi village scene, ca. 1898.

Toson Koyemsi

Wilfred Tewawina
Hopi, ca. 1960–80
SAR.1989-7-15
Height: 8.1 cm
Acquired in 1989

The Toson (Sweet Cornmeal-Tasting) Koyemsi comes dressed like this when he is with the Ogres, or Soyoko. During Powamu, he and Soyok Wuhti (Ogre Woman) visit every house in the village where there are children. The Ogre Woman gives each girl a handful of corn, telling her she must grind it before the Soyoko return in about a week. The Toson Koyemsi passes out small snares made of yucca to the boys and tells them they must trap deer before the return of the Ogres or the monsters will take them. During this visit the Toson Koyemsi has a blanket wrapped about his body and a red bow and an evergreen sprig tied around the central knob on his crown. When he returns with the Ogres, he does not wear a blanket.

When the Soyoko return, the Toson Koyemsi tastes the cornmeal each girl has ground to see if it is sweet. When the boys hold out the mice ("deer") they have trapped, the Ogres roar with disapproval and threaten to take the children away. The children are then forced to rectify any misbehavior by doing whatever the katsinas demand, in front of everyone. Their parents offer corn or meat to ransom the children. All the food is taken by the Toson Koyemsi back to the kiva. At the end of the day the men of the village lure the band of Ogres into a dance, then attack them, retrieve all the ransom, and run them out of town.

The entire performance emphasizes individual responsibility, family support, and village cooperation against malignant outside forces. Although this katsina looks very much like the Koyemshi of Zuni, he has no counterpart in that village. The white, annular mouth and the blue crescent between the eyes are unique. On either cheek the symbol for sprouting beans is painted in blue-green and black. When the Toson Koyemsi comes in this role, he is not a clown but one of the older and more sacred Hopi katsinas. *Barton Wright*

Konin Mana Katsina

Hopi, ca. 1950–70
SAR.1989-7-132
Height: 26.7cm
Acquired in 1989

The Konin Mana (Havasupai Girl) is one of the more beautiful female katsinas. The Hopi like to make katsina impersonations of their neighbors, and the Havasupai are a favorite subject. Their home lies to the west of the Hopi mesas, and the two tribes have been trading for countless years. Hopi katsina impersonations are not copies of individuals but only representations; consequently the Konin Mana does not resemble Havasupai women and girls in either costume or countenance.

The Havasupai dance features the male Konin and his sister, the Konin Mana, a side dancer known as Miyuksola, and a chorus of singers, the Taolaoka. All are masked figures. The same dance can also be given as a social dance by the young men and women, in which the costumes are identical but no masks are worn. Both forms of the dance are quite beautiful to watch, and the songs are very melodic. The Konin Mana carries a basket in her left hand and gestures with it. She places her right hand on her hip with arm akimbo and dances very gracefully.

This rare doll, a gift from Henry Galbraith, wears a full tanned buckskin of the kind usually acquired from the Jicarilla Apaches in New Mexico. She carries a basket done in Hopi coiled work with a Navajo design, often called a Havasupai basket. Her headgear consists of a piece of red yarn adorned with metallic buttons placed across the forehead, with the ends hanging down at either side of the face—a design frequently found in Hopi depictions of Comanches. Horns—symbols of power—are decorated with polychrome bands. These and the multicolored blocks on the face may represent the colors of corn or clouds from the various directions. The underside of the chin is striped with alternating bands of blue and red. This design is a consistent pattern on First Mesa and is absent elsewhere. Normally there is a fan of eagle feathers behind the head or encircling the forehead; occasionally there are only two feathers on either side of the head. *Barton Wright*

"Supai Mana Dance." Painting
by Fred Kabotie, ca. 1921.

Eówing Tsená Katsina

Hopi-Tewa, ca. 1960–80
SAR.1994-8-115
Height: 27cm
Acquired in 1994

Eówing Tsená (Tobacco Clan Old Man, a warrior) is one of four Chief katsinas that the Tewa people brought with them when they emigrated from the Rio Grande to Hopi country around 1703. The others are Ke Towa, Pohaha, and Heheya. Eówing Tsená's name is derived from his call of "Eowi!" ("We are coming!")—although nobody seems to know why he is coming or from where. The Tewa say that Tsena means old man and is a term used for a respected elder, the equivalent of the Hopi term *wuye*, or spiritual partner of a clan. Sometimes the name is written Eówing Sendo, meaning simply Tobacco Clan. His common name is the Tewa Whipper katsina. The Hopi Tumas and Tungwup katsinas initiate children into the Katsina Cult in the kiva during Powamu, but in the Tewa ritual two of the Eówing Tsená whip the children in the plaza.

There are several versions of this katsina. In the one described in 1921 by Elsie Clews Parsons from information given by Angwusi, a Tewa man, the katsina has a roach of snakeweed, two warrior feathers, red ears, globular eyes, an angled white stripe down the face, and a small mouth with a thin beard. He wears a complete suit of buckskin clothing, with a buckskin cape and a cornhusk ruff.

In the 1950s the katsina doll wore buckskin leggings, a black breechcloth, a buckskin wrapped about the waist, another slung over the left shoulder and under the right arm, and a bandolier over the right shoulder. The head was white, with a black angled stripe down the face, and all the other elements were the same. By 1989 the doll wore a buckskin about the waist and over the right shoulder. Its head was half white and half black, separated by an angled red stripe, and its ears were square, with an X through them.

This rare doll, one of a large collection donated by Ruth Holmwood, has a white head divided vertically by a broad black band. It wears knitted full-length stockings, a blue belt over a wrapped buckskin, a black breechcloth, and a buckskin cape. The torso is brown, with two white patches on the chest. *Barton Wright*

Hemis Katsina

Hopi, ca. 1940–50
SAR.1994-8-155
Height: 56cm
Acquired in 1994

The Hemis is one of the better-known Hopi katsinas. Its name supposedly comes from the fact that it was borrowed from the Pueblo of Jemez. However, there is no katsina at Jemez that resembles this one. It shows a much closer visual and ceremonial relationship to the Hemishikwe of Zuni.

The Hemis katsina is most commonly seen during the Niman (Home-Going) ceremony in late July, but it can also appear as one of the Dawn katsinas delivering bean sprouts to the various households during the Powamu ceremony. Because Hemis comes for the Niman ceremony, it is also called the Niman katsina; this is a generic term, as there are other katsinas, such as the Kuwan Heheya, Tasap, and Ma-alo, who may also come as the Niman katsina. Hopi artist Fred Kabotie maintained that the true name of this katsina was the Hümis (Young Corn) katsina, for it is the one that brings in the first corn of the season, but in fact the other Niman katsinas also do so.

The symbols that form the decoration on the Hemis katsina are a repetitive visual supplication for rain. The tableta is cut into a terraced rain cloud. At each right angle is a turkey feather that resembles a storm cloud, and in front of it a sprig of sandgrass, whose seed head looks like corn. Across the face of the tableta rise five long clouds (*wupa omau*), sometimes mistakenly identified as phallic symbols. A rainbow rises above other smaller cloud symbols.

The lower edges of the tableta are painted with small, stacked clouds atop a band of falling rain. The brim above the face is a row of soft white feathers representing clouds. A band down the center of the face has white annulets, the mark of rain falling in pools of water. At the base of the mask are short rainbows, the kind seen in the early morning when the sun shines through the dew on the corn. The ruff and sprigs tucked into the arm and waistbands represent vegetation, and the black body is a symbol of the earth damp with rain. This katsina doll is part of the Ruth Holmwood bequest. *Barton Wright*

"Niman Kachina Dance."
Painting by Fred Kabotie, 1920.

LEATHER
AND
BEADWORK

Dance Moccasins

Zuni Pueblo, ca. 1940
IAF.C292
Height: 19.1cm Length: 26.75cm
Acquired in 1963

The great ceremonial dances of the Pueblo Indians are among the most colorful events in North America. The dancers' brilliant costumes include woven mantas, embroidered skirts and blouses, towering tabletas (wooden headdresses), and elaborate masks. Footwear too is often colored and decorated with paints and appliqué elements. These fine, rare dance moccasins from Zuni are outstanding examples.

Made from a rather thick skin, possibly elk, in the common Southwestern ankle-height style, they are slit up the side and held in place with skin thongs. The foot covering and the upright section around the ankle are made in a single piece. The folded cuffs are colored red and yellow, and a red rectangle hangs on the outside. A thong across the instep holds the moccasin in place, and double flaps of red and yellow cover part of the instep. Red fringe is attached to the back of the upper cuff. The soles are of the usual Southwestern type, made of hard rawhide and turned up slightly around the lower edge of the soft skin uppers. They are painted jet black, and they shine when polished.

The most unusual features of these moccasins are the bands tied around the heels and decorated with porcupine quills. Quill decorations, which are rare in the Southwest, were used on moccasins by both the Zunis and Hopis from about 1880 to 1900. It seems likely that their appearance was inspired by contact with tribes from the Great Plains or the Great Basin. The undyed quills are attached by a Lakota technique called quill-wrapped double-rawhide strips. A strip of stiff rawhide is slit into several pairs of narrow strips, and white quills are wrapped around each pair, held in place by sinew threads that twine in and out of the quills. Dark horsehairs create simple X designs. The finished strip is sewn to a backing of heavy red wool with colored yarn embroidery. Similar decorations are used today, but they are now made with colored trade yarn. *Andrew Hunter Whiteford*

Beaded Cradle

Kiowa, ca. 1885
IAF.M320
Length: 115.6cm Width: 33.6cm
Acquired in 1942

Many North American Indian tribes made elegant cradles, but none surpassed those of the Kiowa of the Southern Plains in their colors, their elaborately beaded decorations, and the design of their construction. In this typical Kiowa cradle, very small trade beads cover the entire surface of the soft buckskin bag in tightly sewn spot stitching. The boldly colored designs are different on the two sides. A flaring hood of stiff rawhide, to shield the infant, tops the bag; additional protection is provided by the stiff lattice framework of polished wood, to which the cradle is attached with buckskin thongs. The long, pointed extensions above the cradle protect the baby's head if the cradle should fall from the mother's horse. They also allow the cradle to be propped up against a tree while the mother does her work.

The simplified floral or leaf designs seen here, characteristic of the Kiowa, are composed largely of diamond shapes in a variety of arrangements. The varicolored borders make them stand out on the dark green background, and the total composition is meticulously balanced even though the two sides of the cradle are entirely different from each other. This outstanding example was collected before 1900 by W. A. L. Thompson in Kansas or Oklahoma and donated to the Indian Arts Fund by his granddaughter, Nancy Thompson.

Andrew Hunter Whiteford

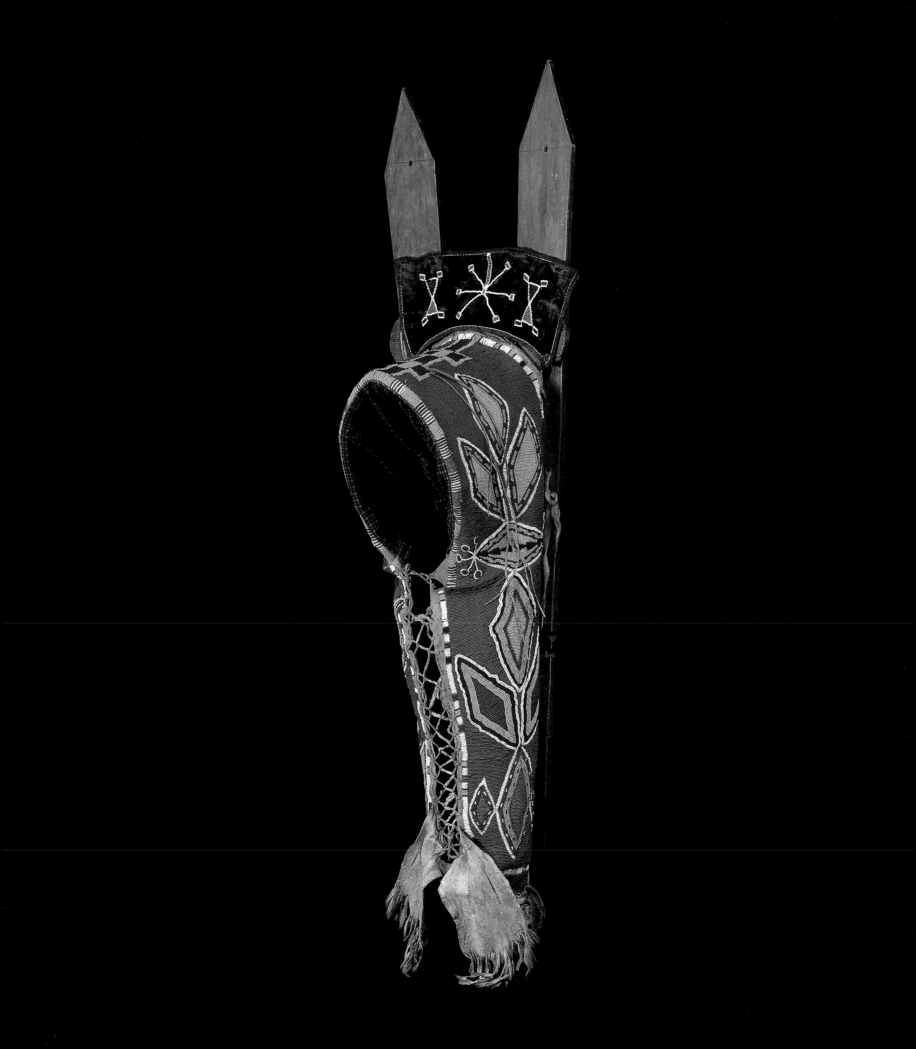

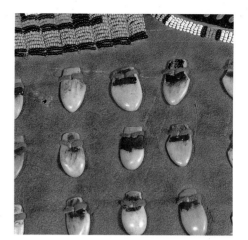

Woman's Deerskin Dress
Arapaho, ca. 1895
IAF.M467
Length: 114.3cm
Acquired in 1963

Famed as warriors, horsemen, great hunters, and skilled craftsmen, the Arapaho Indians epitomize the early tribes of the Southern Plains. Like their longtime allies, the Cheyennes, they speak an Algonquian language. Both groups moved south around 1865 to settle on reservations in Oklahoma Territory. This beautiful dress is a fine example of the style worn in the Southern Plains by Cheyenne, Kiowa, and Comanche women. It consists of a blouse made of two soft skins of doe or antelope, and a long skirt of two deerskins or elkskins sewn together along the edges.

Among the Southern Plains Indians, paint and fringe were more important decorations than beadwork. Here, yellow ochre paint covers the blouse, which also features a strip of beadwork on each shoulder, a narrow band of red trade cloth around the neck opening, a mass of long fringe at the ends of the short sleeves, and five horizontal rows of imitation elk teeth. The shoulder strips are decorated with small porcelain trade beads in vertical bands of lazy stitching to form three yellow rectangles framed in dark blue on a light blue ground. The "elk teeth," important symbols of wealth, are skillfully carved from heavy bone and colored to look more realistic. The long fringe on the sleeves is unusually thick and heavy for the Southern Plains. The tailoring is skillful, with sinew stitching hidden in the seams. The seam where the skirt and blouse are sewn together is covered with an additional strip of skin, and the join between sleeve and blouse is finished with a scalloped edge painted pink.

The skirt has a short fringe down the edges and a longer fringe along the straight hemline, ending in undecorated pointed pendants at each side. Just above the hem is a broad band painted a deep, ochre red. On the front and back of the skirt are two red-and-blue beaded rectangles, each with a large, shiny, German-silver boss in the middle. Although this dress resembles classic Cheyenne dresses in some ways, it lacks such typical Cheyenne features as beaded crossbands, decorated corner pendants on the skirt, and a scalloped border of beads and paint above the hemline. *Andrew Hunter Whiteford*

Girl's Ceremonial Dress

Mescalero Apache, ca. 1930
IAF.M482
Length: Blouse, 61cm; skirt, 97cm
Acquired in 1963

When an Apache girl reaches maturity, she undergoes a four-day Sunrise ceremony. With guidance, prayers, and invocations to the gods through dances and songs, she is initiated into full status as a woman of the tribe and of her clan. Guests and participants receive gifts of food, baskets, and even horses. The total enterprise is very expensive, often running to thousands of dollars. One of the most important elements of the Sunrise ceremony is the traditional dress worn by the girl, usually made by a member of the family. The Mescalero dress shown here is a classic example.

Unlike the one-piece dresses of many tribes, Apache dresses are made in two separate sections—a short, poncho-like blouse, which is pulled on over the head, and a skirt that ties around the waist and hangs to the ankles. Five complete deerskins are required: one for the blouse, two for the skirt, and two more for the long fringes.

The dresses are fluid when worn, primarily because of the very long, fine fringes hanging from the shoulders and all around the skirt. On this dress the fringe is enhanced with orange

Jeannette Larzelere on the last day of her puberty ceremony. Whiteriver, Fort Apache reservation, 1984.

and dark green coloring. The rich colors were achieved by grinding malachite for the green and limonite for the yellow; the pigments were then mixed with yucca juice and grease so they could be rubbed into the soft buckskin. The edge of the green bib and the bottom of the blouse are fringed with hundreds of tin "tinklers," usually made from the lids of cans. Small groups of cones hanging from the front of the blouse also tinkle when the wearer walks or dances. Further decoration is provided by lines of white beads.

This dress was a gift from Elizabeth White, who probably acquired it for the Indian art gallery she owned in New York in the 1920s and 1930s. *Andrew Hunter Whiteford*

Woman's Awl Case

Apache, ca. 1875
SAR.1978-1-38
Height: 48.3cm Width: 6.4cm
Acquired in 1978

No tool was more important to an Apache woman than the awl that she carried on her belt in a fitted skin case and used for making baskets and sewing and decorating buckskin dresses, shirts, and moccasins. Awls had needlelike metal points set into handles of carved wood, bone, or antler. They made perforations through which threads of sinew were passed. Carrying cases for awls were carefully decorated, but few were as distinctive as the one shown here,

This awl case, part of Elizabeth White's estate, is in a classic style that was unique to the Western Apache and has not been made for many years. The lower beaded disk marks the end of the actual case; the ends of the painted yellow cover are divided into two elongated triangles that hang free. Small trade beads were sewn onto the two disks and in a vertical row of blue chevrons on the hanging flaps. Both for visual beauty and the music they produced, tin tinklers were attached in a line across the upper section and along the edges. They would swing as the woman moved. *Andrew Hunter Whiteford*

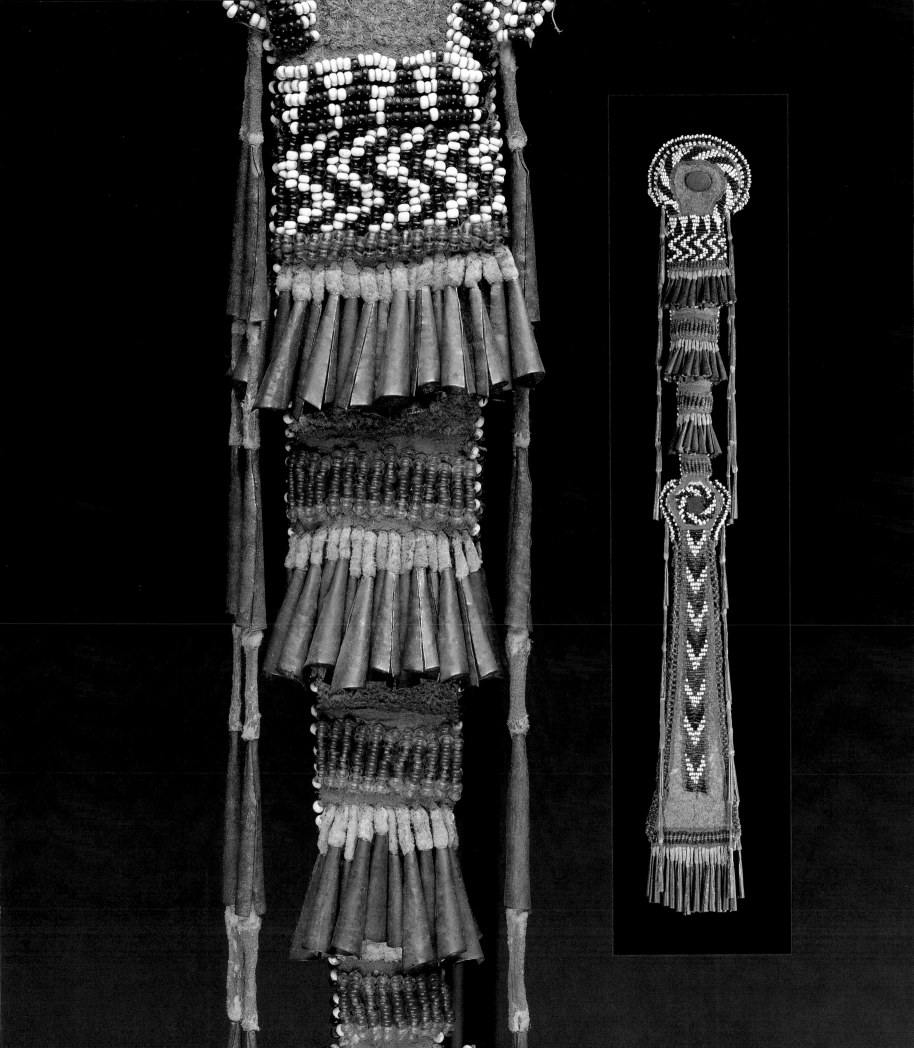

Plains Shield

Cheyenne, ca. 1900
SAR.1978-1-86
Length: 130cm Width: 48cm
Acquired in 1978

Traditionally, men of the Cheyenne and other Great Plains tribes devoted most of their lives to hunting and warfare. Generosity and bravery were the supreme virtues, signified by the wearing of special feathers, shirts, and other socially approved regalia. A Plains warrior's most important possession was the semisacred, decorated shield that he carried. Before 1880 such shields provided protection in battle, in part through their sacred power, in part because the buffaloskin with which they were made had been shrunk to a thickness of half an inch and could ward off arrows and even musketballs.

The advent of rifle bullets ended the basic utility of the shields, but they continued to be regarded as articles of great power and status. By 1900 shields like the one illustrated here were being made especially for men of status to carry during ceremonial dances. Lighter and thinner than the old buffaloskin shields, they were often painted with significant designs.

This shield was one of Elizabeth White's favorite pieces and hung on the wall of her Santa Fe bedroom. It is made with two thin rawhide disks, laced together around the edges and enclosed in a fine buckskin cover that is painted a soft orange, with a beaded band along the upper edge. The cover has a beaded disk at its center, eagle plumes tipped with "fluffies" (short feathers from the eagle's back and neck), and four broad streamers of red wool strouding (tradecloth) that hang on each side of the shield. The plumes and streamers provide very effective decoration while the owner is dancing. The shield appears to be Cheyenne in its structure and decoration and is a fine example of the continuation of an old custom into the twentieth century. *Andrew Hunter Whiteford*

Warrior with shield. Southern Cheyenne drawing, Frederic H. Douglas ledger, ca. 1870.

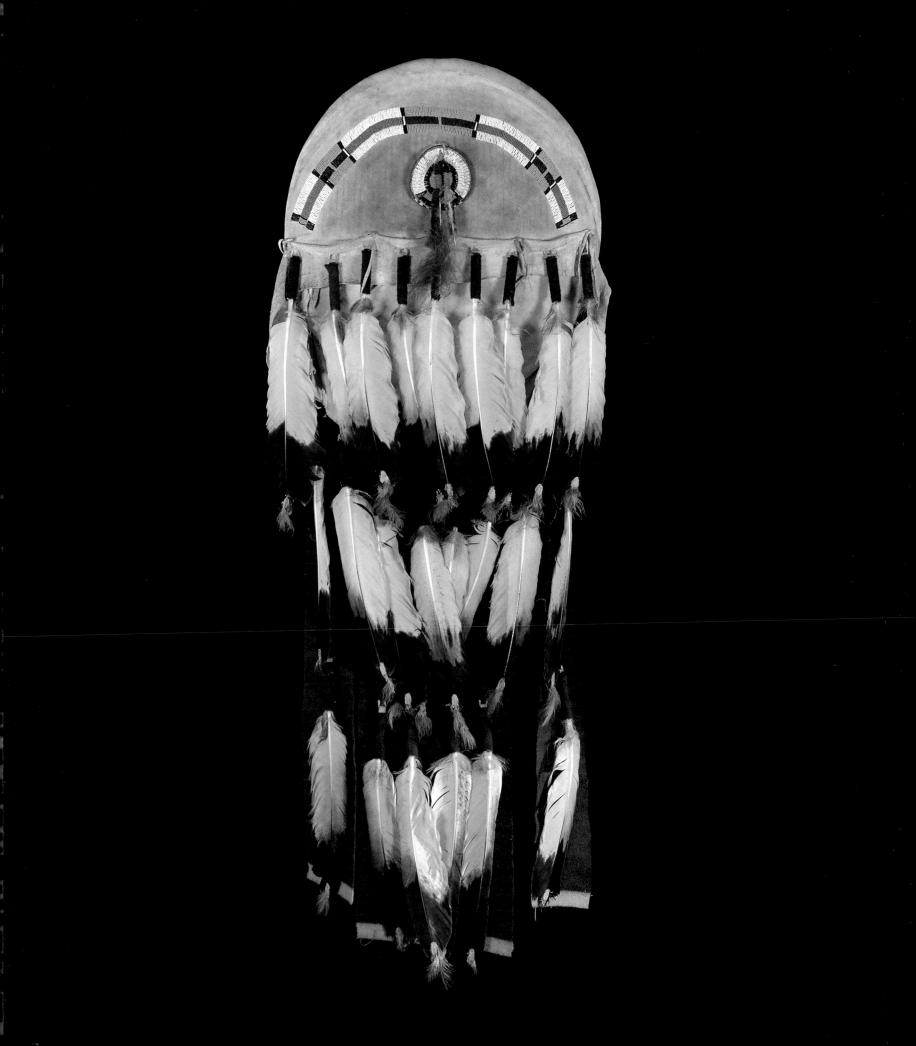

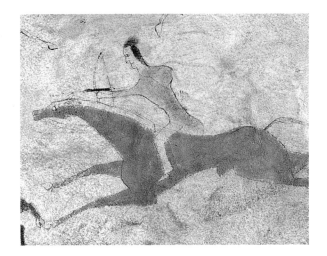

Painted Elkskin

Katsikodi
Shoshone, ca. 1890
SAR.1978-1-87
Height: 160cm Width: 160cm
Acquired in 1978

Men of the Great Plains tribes painted their robes and tipi covers with images of their exploits in battle and other important ceremonial events. This elkskin painting depicts a great buffalo hunt and a Sun Dance ceremony. The artist, Katsikodi or Tinzoni, a Shoshone from Wind River, Wyoming, was recorded in the tribal roll of 1900 as Cadzi Cody (Codsiogo). He was born about 1866 and died in 1912. Thus he would have witnessed the last of the great buffalo hunts and almost certainly would have participated in the Sun Dance.

Katsikodi's twenty-odd known paintings portray horses in many positions and hunters killing buffalo and carving up their carcasses. In this painting, the fleeing bison are so alike that it is possible that the artist used patterns or even stencils for their outlines. At the center are men seated around a drum and prancing dancers gathered around a pole. In the middle of the nineteenth century, when the Sun Dance was prohibited, the pole would display the American flag, but after 1890 the religious Sun Dance was allowed, and the central pole once again was topped with a buffalo head or a spread-winged eagle.

In Katsikodi's work, a traditional art form was adapted to a changing life pattern. His paintings depicted aspects of the old life but were created for sale to tourists who came to see the Sun Dance and collect distinctive souvenirs. This painting was featured in Douglas and d'Harnoncourt's *Indian Art of the United States* (1941), one of the first books to be published on American Indian art. *Andrew Hunter Whiteford*

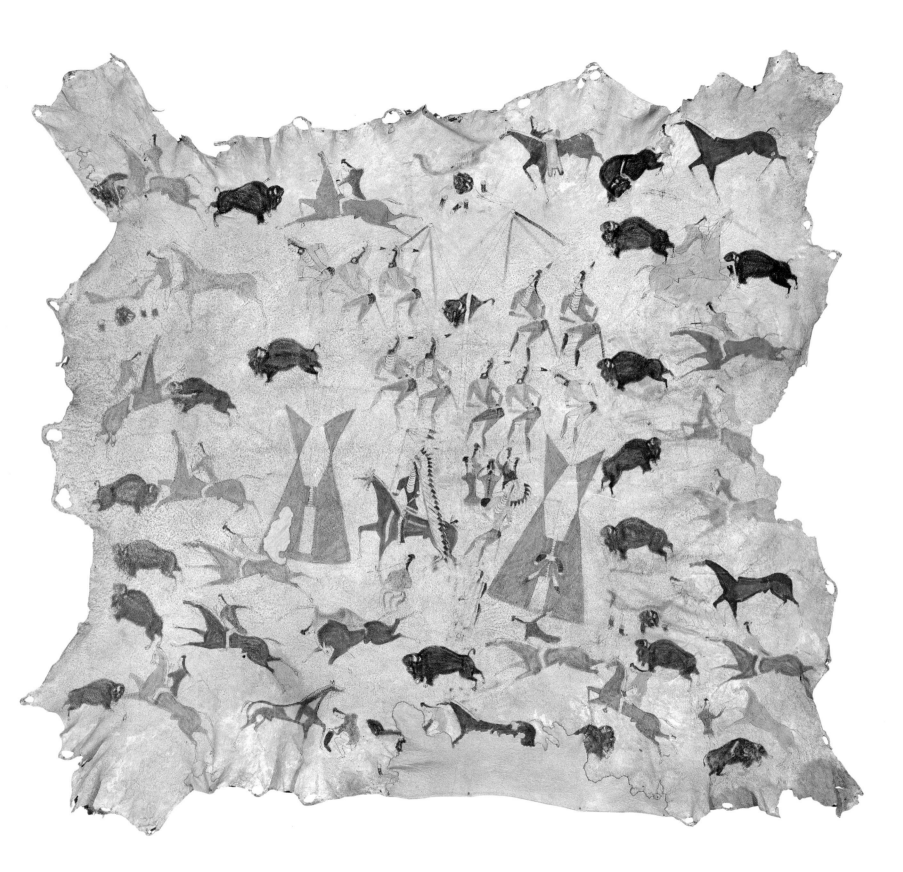

Rawhide Saddlebags

Western Apache, ca. 1875
SAR.1984-4-44
Length: 194cm Width: 38.5cm
Acquired in 1984

The Western Apaches decorated their buckskin clothing with beads, porcupine quills, and painted designs, and with perforated designs that were cut through the skin. The latter technique, widespread among Plains groups, was elaborated by the Apaches, who cut complex designs in sheets of stiff rawhide, allowing colored tradecloth to show through.
This was a favorite mode of decorating large saddlebags.

Measuring more than six feet long, this typical Western Apache bag contains two compartments that open through the longitudinal slit between them. Each is decorated with a rectangular panel, cut to create three rows of circular figures with stars or diamonds at their centers. The designs are backed by red wool tradecloth. The ends of the rawhide have deep lobes with circles cut in their centers so they appear to be rings; these sections too are backed with red cloth. Beyond the rawhide section at each end is a rectangle of soft buckskin, framed with yellow bands on the sides and top and strung with six groups of three or four tin tinklers. The skin section between the side bands is cut into long strands of fringe.
Andrew Hunter Whiteford

White Mountain Apache camp, ca. 1906.

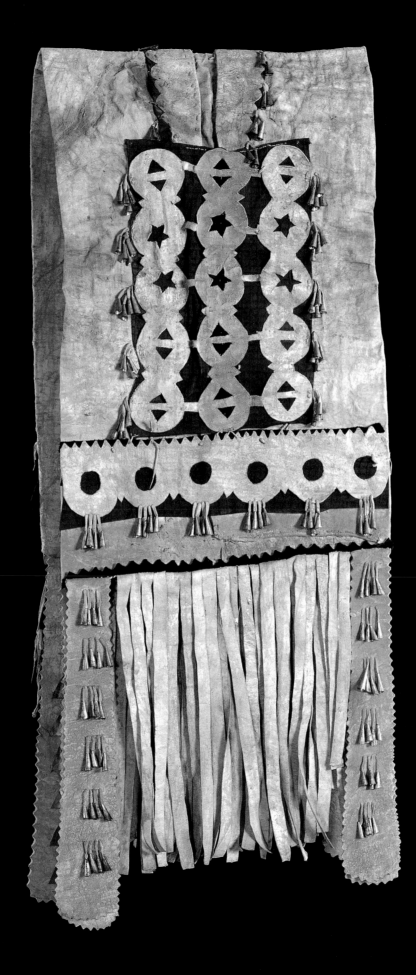

ACKNOWLEDGMENTS

This book was made possible by the generosity of the *Legacy* patrons, whose passion for the subject matter parallels that of the celebrated collectors of the original Indian Arts Fund. Snooky and Blake Blakemore, co-chairs of the *Legacy* fund drive, participated enthusiastically in the campaign and graciously allowed us to use their home for fund-raising events. Thanks go also to Charles M. Diker, who provided seed money for a book about the Indian art collection at the School of American Research two years before president Douglas Schwartz launched the project as part of the School's observance of its ninetieth anniversary.

We were fortunate in recruiting an outstanding group of scholars to write the brief essays on individual objects. Barbara A. Babcock, Jonathan Batkin, Allison Bird-Romero, J. J. Brody, Jill Leslie McKeever Furst, Margaret Ann Hardin, Francis H. Harlow, Barbara Kramer, Susan Brown McGreevy, Marian Rodee, Andrew Hunter Whiteford, and Barton Wright willingly shared their time and expertise. I couldn't have asked for better colleagues to assist with the project.

At the Indian Arts Research Center, Michael J. Hering helped select objects and solicit manuscripts, and assisted with the preparation of the text. Deborah Dodge Winton kept master lists of items to be featured, tracked submissions by authors, and compiled automated revisions of the manuscript. Project conservator Bettina Raphael provided advice on the handling and care of the artifacts and did an excellent job of preparing specimens for the photographer. Christy Sturm, assisted by Ron Martinez Looking Elk and Daryl Candelaria, helped with the selection and tracking of objects, compiled records for the authors, and facilitated conservation and photography.

At the SAR Press, project designer Deborah Flynn Post, one of the early proponents of a book about the Indian art collections, assisted with item selection, supervised the photographic process, helped locate supporting visual materials, and contributed a wealth of ideas that greatly improved the final product. Joan O'Donnell, director of the Press, helped formulate the *Legacy* concept, participated in the selection of objects, commented on numerous draft manuscripts, and facilitated the overall editorial process. All of the authors are indebted to Jo Ann Baldinger, copy editor, for her skillful handling of the entire manuscript; she managed to make the text flow while preserving the individual quality of each author's contribution.

This book would not be as beautiful, striking, or exciting as it is without the inspired work of our primary photographer, Addison Doty, who painstakingly staged each shot to bring out the desired qualities of the subject.

Finally, I am grateful to N. Scott Momaday, a member of the School's Board of Managers and a former SAR resident scholar, for his inspirational Foreword. It sets the tone from the Native American perspective in a way that honors the legacy theme and reminds us that the real credit for this book must go to the talent and creativity of Native Americans who have been producing outstanding art for centuries.

Duane Anderson
Vice President
School of American Research

CONTRIBUTORS

DUANE ANDERSON is vice president of the School of American Research. He received his Ph.D. from the University of Colorado, where he specialized in the archaeology of the Southwest and Midwest. He has published research papers in the fields of archaeology, ethnohistory, paleontology, and museum studies, and is the author of two popular books. He recently completed *All That Glitters*, a study of the micaceous pottery traditions of northern New Mexico, which will be published by SAR Press.

BARBARA A. BABCOCK is Regents Professor of English and graduate advisor of the Program in Comparative Cultural and Literary Studies at the University of Arizona, with a joint appointment in Indian Studies. Her numerous publications on Southwestern anthropology, the invention of the Southwest, and Pueblo art include *The Pueblo Storyteller: Development of a Figurative Ceramic Tradition* (1986). She is presently completing a study of Cochiti potter Helen Cordero and a collection of critical essays on the politics of representation.

JONATHAN BATKIN, director of the Wheelwright Museum of the American Indian in Santa Fe, was formerly co-director and chief curator of the Southwest Museum, Los Angeles, and curator of the Taylor Museum in Colorado Springs. A research curator of the School of American Research and vice president of the Native American Art Studies Association, Batkin is the author of *Pottery of the Pueblos of New Mexico, 1700–1940* and numerous articles on Pueblo pottery and other Native American arts. He received his M.A. in anthropology from the University of Denver.

ALLISON BIRD-ROMERO is an independent scholar and research curator at the School of American Research. She is the author of *Heart of the Dragonfly: The Historical Development of Cross Necklaces of the Pueblo and Navajo Peoples* (1993) and co-author of *In the Spirit of the Ancestors: The Kappmeyer Collection of Native American Art* (1997). She is currently working on a biography of Zuni Pueblo trader C. E. Wallace and other Zuni traders active from 1860 to 1940.

J. J. BRODY is professor emeritus of art history at the University of New Mexico and former director of its Maxwell Museum of Anthropology. His major research and teaching interests are in American Indian art and museology. His books include *Indian Painters and White Patrons* (1970), *Mimbres Painted Pottery* (1977), *Anasazi and Pueblo Painting* (1991), and *Pueblo Indian Painting: Tradition and Modernism in New Mexico, 1900–1930* (1997). He has also organized numerous museum exhibitions.

JILL LESLIE MCKEEVER FURST received her M.A. from the University of Colorado and her Ph.D. from the University of New Mexico. She is professor of art history at Moore College of Art and Design, Philadelphia, and a consult-

ing scholar in the American section of the University of Pennsylvania Museum. She is the author of *The Natural History of the Soul in Ancient Mexico* (1995) and co-author *of North American Indian Art* (1982).

MARGARET ANN HARDIN is curator and section head of the program in anthropology at the Natural History Museum of Los Angeles County and a research associate of the Heritage and Historic Preservation Office of the Pueblo of Zuni. She earned her master's and Ph.D. degrees from the University of Chicago and is the author of *Gifts of Mother Earth: Ceramics in the Zuni Tradition* (1983).

FRANCIS H. HARLOW, a Fellow of the Los Alamos National Laboratory, holds a Ph.D. in theoretical physics from the University of Washington and has published research papers in the fields of physics, applied mathematics, and engineering. He is the author or co-author of six books and numerous articles on the history of Pueblo Indian pottery and is a frequent lecturer in this field.

MICHAEL J. HERING is director of the Indian Arts Research Center at the School of American Research. He holds an M.A. in Native American Arts from the University of New Mexico and is a graduate of the J. Paul Getty Trust's Museum Management Institute. Hering received a National Endowment for the Arts Fellowship for his research on Zia Pueblo pottery.

BARBARA KRAMER is an independent scholar who writes frequently about the arts and the lives of individual artists for numerous publications and reference books. Her extensive research on the Hopi-Tewa potter Nampeyo produced the first complete biographical narrative and stylistic analysis of Nampeyo and her work. Kramer's book *Nampeyo and Her Pottery* was published by the University of New Mexico Press in 1996.

SUSAN BROWN MCGREEVY, who received her M.A. in anthropology from Northwestern University, is a research associate and former director of the Wheelwright Museum of the American Indian. She is a contributing co-editor of *Washington Matthews: Studies of Navajo Culture 1880–1894* (1997) and author of "The Story Tellers: Contemporary Navajo Basket Makers" (1996), "What Makes Sally Weave: Survival and Innovation in Navajo Basketry Trays" (1989), and *The Image Weavers: Contemporary Navajo Pictorial Textiles* (1994).

N. SCOTT MOMADAY is a novelist, poet, and playwright, and winner of the 1969 Pulitzer Prize in fiction for *House Made of Dawn*. His other books include *The Way to Rainy Mountain* (1969), *The Names* (1976), and *The Man Made of Words* (1997). A member of the Kiowa tribe of Oklahoma, Momaday lives in Jemez Springs, New Mexico, and is Regent's Professor of English at the University of Arizona.

MARIAN RODEE is curator of Southwestern ethnology at the University of New Mexico's Maxwell Museum of Anthropology. She holds a B.A. in anthropology from the University of Pennsylvania and a master's degree in classical archaeology from Columbia University. Rodee has published several books and articles on Navajo weaving, including a catalog of the Maxwell Museum's textile collection entitled *Weaving of the Southwest* (1987).

ANDREW HUNTER "BUD" WHITEFORD, former director of the Logan Museum of Anthropology, is professor emeritus of anthropology at Beloit College, a research curator at the School of American Research, and a research associate at the Wheelwright Museum of the American Indian. He serves on the advisory board of *American Indian Art Magazine* and has published numerous articles and books, including *North American Indian Arts* (1970) and *Southwestern Indian Baskets: Their History and Their Makers* (1988).

BARTON WRIGHT is a former curator and assistant director of the Museum of Northern Arizona in Flagstaff and also served as scientific director of San Diego's Museum of Man. He is the author of numerous books on Southwestern subjects such as katsinas, Hopi material culture, Pueblo shields, and Zuni mythology. He holds a master's degree from the University of Arizona.

SELECTED BIBLIOGRAPHY

Amon Carter Museum of Western Art
1966   Quiet Triumph: Forty Years with the
        Indian Arts Fund, Santa Fe. Amon Carter
        Museum, Fort Worth.

Amsden, Charles Avery
1949   Navajo Weaving. University of New
        Mexico Press, Albuquerque.

Anderson, Duane
In Press   All That Glitters: Native American
        Micaceous Pottery of Northern New
        Mexico. School of American Research
        Press, Santa Fe.

Anderson, Duane, and John Ware
n.d.   The Native American Micaceous Pottery
        Traditions of Northern New Mexico:
        1880–1998. Unpublished manuscript.

Batkin, Jonathan
1987a   Martina Vigil and Florentino Montoya:
        Master Potters of San Ildefonso and
        Cochiti Pueblos. *American Indian Art
        Magazine* 12(4), Autumn.

1987b   Pottery of the Pueblos of New Mexico:
        1700–1940. Colorado Springs Fine Arts
        Center, Colorado Springs.

1991   Three Great Potters of San Ildefonso
        and Their Legacy. *American Indian Art
        Magazine* 16(4), Autumn.

Bird, Allison
1993   Jewelry Collection at the School of
        American Research. *American Indian Art
        Magazine* 18(4), Autumn.

Blair, Mary Ellen, and Laurence Blair
1986   Margaret Tafoya: A Tewa Potter's
        Heritage and Legacy. Schiffer Publishing
        Ltd., West Chester, PA.

Brako, Jeanne, and Bob Morgan
1987   Conservation: Navajo Textiles. *American
        Indian Art Magazine* 12(3), Summer.

Brody, J. J.
1971   Indian Painters and White Patrons.
        University of New Mexico Press,
        Albuquerque.

1997   Pueblo Indian Painting: Tradition and
        Modernism in New Mexico, 1900–1930.
        School of American Research Press,
        Santa Fe.

Bunzel, Ruth
1929   The Pueblo Potter: A Study of Creative
        Imagination in Primitive Art. Contributions
        to Anthropology, vol. 7. Columbia
        University, New York.

Chapman, Kenneth M.
1938   The Pottery of Santo Domingo Pueblo.
        Revised in 1953. University of New
        Mexico Press and the School of American
        Research, Albuquerque and Santa Fe.

1970   The Pottery of San Ildefonso Pueblo.
        University of New Mexico Press and the
        School of American Research,
        Albuquerque and Santa Fe.

Crown, Patricia L., and W. James Judge
1991   Chaco and Hohokam: Prehistoric Regional
        Systems in the American Southwest.
        School of American Research Press,
        Santa Fe.

Dillingham, Rick
1984   The Ceramic Collection of the School of
        American Research, Santa Fe, New
        Mexico. The Studio Potter 12(2):74–80.

1992   Acoma & Laguna Pottery. School of
        American Research Press, Santa Fe.

1994   Fourteen Families in Pueblo Pottery.
        University of New Mexico Press,
        Albuquerque.

Dittert, Alfred E., and Fred Plog
1980   Generations in Clay: Pueblo Pottery of
        the American Southwest. Northland Press,
        Flagstaff.

Douglas, Frederic H., and René d'Harnoncourt
1941   Indian Art of the United States. Museum
        of Modern Art, New York.

Fox, Nancy
1978   Pueblo Weaving and Textile Arts.
        Guidebook no. 3. Museum of New
        Mexico Press, Santa Fe.

Frank, Larry, and Francis H. Harlow
1974   Historic Pottery of the Pueblo Indians,
        1600–1880. New York Graphic Society,
        Boston.

Furst, Jill Leslie McKeever
In Press Mojave Pottery. School of American
        Research Press, Santa Fe.

Harlow, Francis H.
1970   Historic Pueblo Indian Pottery. Museum of
        New Mexico Press, Santa Fe.

1973   Matte-Paint Pottery of the Tewa, Keres,
        and Zuni Pueblos. Museum of New
        Mexico Press, Santa Fe.

Hering, Michael J.
1987   Zia Matte-Paint Pottery: A 300-Year
        History. American Indian Art Magazine
        12(4), Autumn.

Irving, David
1987   Kate Peck Kent and the Study of Historic
        Pueblo Textiles. Wheelwright Museum of
        the American Indian, Santa Fe.

James, George Wharton
1927   Indian Blankets and Their Makers. A. C.
        McClurg Co., Chicago.

Kent, Kate Peck
1983   Pueblo Indian Textiles: A Living Tradition. School of American Research Press, Santa Fe.

1985   Navajo Weaving: Three Centuries of Change. School of American Research Press, Santa Fe.

LeFree, Betty
1975   Santa Clara Pottery Today. University of New Mexico Press, Albuquerque.

Levy, Jerrold E.
1992   Orayvi Revisited: Social Stratification in an "Egalitarian" Society. School of American Research Press, Santa Fe.

Mera, H. P.
1932–45 Various bulletins on Pueblo pottery and Navajo weaving. Laboratory of Anthropology, Santa Fe.

1938   The Rain Bird: A Study in Pueblo Design. Laboratory of Anthropology, Santa Fe.

1939   Style Trends of Pueblo Pottery in the Rio Grande and Little Colorado Cultural Areas from the Sixteenth Century to the Nineteenth Century. Baltimore Waverly Press, Inc., Santa Fe.

1943   Pueblo Indian Embroidery. *Memoirs of the Laboratory of Anthropology*, vol. IV, Laboratory of Anthropology, Santa Fe.

1947   Navajo Textile Arts. Laboratory of Anthropology, Santa Fe.

1987   Spanish American Blanketry. School of American Research Press, Santa Fe.

Peterson, Susan
1984   Lucy M. Lewis: American Indian Potter. Kodansha International, Tokyo.

1997   Pottery by American Indian Women: The Legacy of Generations. Abbeville Press and the National Museum of Women in the Arts, Washington, D.C.

Spivey, Richard L.
1989   Maria. Northland Publishing Company, Flagstaff.

Trimble, Stephen
1987   Talking with the Clay: The Art of Pueblo Pottery. School of American Research Press, Santa Fe.

Whiteford, Andrew H.
1988   Southwestern Indian Baskets: Their History and Their Makers. School of American Research Press, Santa Fe.

Whiteford, Andrew H., and Susan Brown McGreevy
1985   Translating Tradition: Basketry Arts of the San Juan Paiutes. *American Indian Art Magazine* 11(1), Winter.

PICTURE CREDITS

All photographs in this book are by Addison Doty unless otherwise noted below, and all belong to the School of American Research unless otherwise noted.

ABBREVIATIONS
MNMPA: Museum of New Mexico Photo Archives
SAR: School of American Research

i, Kenneth Chapman; v, Otis Imboden; vii, Kenneth Chapman; xi, Lynn Lown; xiii, Rod Hook; 1, Kenneth Chapman; 3, Herbert Lotz; 4, Mack Photo Service; 5, Laura Gilpin; 6, Mark Nohl; 7, Kay Bynum; 8, Harold Kellogg; 9, photographer unknown; 10, Susan Latham; 11 (all), Rod Hook; 12 (both), Katrina Lasko; 13, Mark Nohl; 14, Rod Hook; 15, 16, Mark Nohl; 17, Otis Imboden.

POTTERY
20, Laura Gilpin, © Amon Carter Museum, Fort Worth, Texas, P1979.149.77, bequest of Laura Gilpin; 24, Kenneth Chapman; 28, Deborah Flynn; 30, Kenneth Chapman; 32, Deborah Flynn; 34, Clyde Fisher; 40, photographer unknown; 42, Deborah Flynn; 44, A. C. Vroman, courtesy of the Southwest Museum, Los Angeles, neg. no. 4320; 46, Rod Hook; 50, Katrina Lasko; 54, Murrae Haynes; 60, SAR Collections in the MNMPA, neg. no. 15956; 62, Herbert Lotz; 64, Sallie Wagner; 68, Susan Latham, courtesy Susan Latham/*The New Mexican*.

PAINTINGS
71, IARC P113, Lynn Lown; 72, photographer unknown, courtesy MNMPA, neg. no. 3742; 74, Parker Hamilton, courtesy Museum of Northern Arizona Photo Archives, neg. no. 2485; 76, photographer unknown, courtesy MNMPA, neg. no. 86519; 80, Witter Bynner, courtesy MNMPA, neg. no. 95264; 82, Wesley Bradfield, courtesy MNMPA, neg. no. 42213; 84, Katrina Lasko; 86, Deborah Flynn; 88, T. Harmon Parkhurst, courtesy MNMPA, neg. no. 46988; 90, David Grant Noble.

TEXTILES
96, 98, Rod Hook; 100, Bureau of American Ethnology, Smithsonian Institution, neg. no. F5894;

101, Darrell Rice; 102, T. Harmon Parkhurst, courtesy MNMPA, neg. no. 3940; 104, courtesy John Galvin; 106, T. Harmon Parkhurst, courtesy Wheelwright Museum of the American Indian; 108, Rod Hook; 110, photographer unknown, SAR Collections in the MNMPA, neg. no. 16479; 112, Deborah Flynn; 116, Rod Hook; 118, SAR.1983-12-148; 122, Katrina Lasko.

BASKETS
126, drawing by Arminta Neal, in Whiteford (1988); 128, Vincent Foster; 132, C. C. Pierce, courtesy of the Southwest Museum, Los Angeles, neg. no. 32370; 136, Laurence Herold, courtesy Photo Archives, Denver Museum of Natural History, all rights reserved; 138, SAR.1993-2-3; 140, SAR.1981-12-2; 142, Deborah Flynn; 146, Rod Hook; 148, Katrina Lasko.

JEWELRY
152, H. F. Robinson; 154, SAR Chapman Archives; 156, Ben Wittick, SAR Collection in the MNMPA, neg. no. 15930; 158, Mark Nohl; 162, John N. Choate, courtesy Denver Public Library, Western History Collection; 166, Mark Nohl.

KATSINAS
176, SAR.1978-1-54; 186, Kenneth Chapman; 190, SAR.1989-21-39; 194, IARC.P22.

LEATHER AND BEADWORK
204, Stephen Trimble; 208, courtesy Canfield Gallery, Santa Fe; 212, Edward S. Curtis, courtesy Arizona State Museum.